Teaching Writing With
Mentor Texts
In The Primary Classroom

By
Nicole Groeneweg

The Very Hungry Caterpillar by Eric Carle

Some Smug Slug by Pamela Duncan Edwards

Pumpkins by Ann L. Burckhardt

Amelia's Notebook by Marissa Moss

Strega Nona by Tomie dePaola

Cara by Patricia Hubbell

Under My Nose by Lois Ehlert

Honey Makers by Gail Gibbons

The Memory String by Eve Bunting

The Hat by Jan Brett

The Wolf's Chicken Stew by Keiko Kasza

■ SCHOLASTIC

New York • Toronto • London • Auckland • Sydney
Mexico City • New Delhi • Hong Kong • Buenos Aires

Cover design and artwork by Jorge J. Namerow
Interior design by Teresa B. Southwell
Interior photographs by Nicole Groeneweg
Edited by Joanna Davis-Swing and Rebecca DeAngelis Callan
ISBN 978-0-545-11593-3
Copyright © 2011 Nicole Groeneweg
All rights reserved.
Printed in the U.S.A.

2 3 4 5 6 7 8 9 10   40   18 17 16 15 14 13 12 11

Table of Contents

Introduction

Think back to your childhood. Did you have someone you revered and then in turn modeled your thinking or behavior after? Most of us have had a mentor at one time or another. Our parents were our earliest role models, and as we grew, we learned from teachers and then experts in our fields of study. Many people have achieved their greatness by having mentors who enhanced their lives.

Several seasoned teachers guided me through the early years of my teaching career. As a trusted colleague, Judy became my mentor. She advised me, she modeled for me, and she was there when I needed a helping hand. I learned how to teach by observing excellent teaching in action. I detailed my observations in a composition book and have referred to them often through the years. Without Judy and other mentors, I would not be the teacher I am today.

As one of the first instructors of Fairfax County's Great Beginnings Program, an induction course dedicated to coaching beginning teachers through their first years of teaching, I in turn became a mentor. I modeled professional teaching standards, provided support and ongoing program assessment, and facilitated classroom-based teacher learning. I felt affirmation that the influence of others certainly makes a difference.

Young writers can turn to experts, too, in our school libraries and our classroom shelves, which veritably burst with examples of great writing. Students can delve into the texts of picture books to investigate characteristics of the writer's craft. That's where some key teachable moments reside, at a pivotal place where students explore and emulate mentor text and where we can guide their efforts and developing skills as emerging writers.

Creating the Literary Environment

One needs to make purposeful choices when molding a stimulating literary environment. To begin, we can provide a writing center or Writers' Corner, rich with literature of all kinds. Beyond that, we need to invite students to participate in the organization of their learning space. Their input is crucial. Here is a glimpse into my child-centered writing environment.

Book Baskets That Go Beyond

By the end of the year, my classroom's Writers' Corner is chock full of writing resources. Labeled baskets overflow with information about mentor authors and their texts. Identified by the author's name and the writing skill learned, each basket holds books that the children determined were good sources of mentor text. Specific passages that were used by students to help them write are marked with bookmarks, sticky arrows, or highlight tape. Notes students have written for their peers about the mentor text are attached to the books. The marked passages and notes become references for other children as they use the center.

The baskets also contain biographical information about the author. This information can be found on author Web sites, in autobiographies, on book jackets, and on mini posters from various book clubs. Other items housed in the baskets may include student-made books inspired by mentor text, photos of charts created during mini lessons, and photos of the authors.

Lessons Learned

We record and celebrate what we've learned from mentor authors in my classroom. As a group, students write short summaries or blurbs of what a mentor author has taught us about a particular craft. These are dictated by the students using their own language. Typically we write them during or after each mentor-text mini lesson. All the blurbs are posted in easy-to-see spots near the Writers' Corner. Here is one of the blurbs my students wrote:

Writers use alliteration to make sentences sound interesting. Alliteration is using the same beginning sounds over and over again in the same sentence or story.

Homespun Definitions

To post a writing process chart in a classroom is not enough. Students must understand each stage of the writing process. By guiding and allowing the students themselves to define each stage, we can better ensure true comprehension.

For example, after practicing many prewriting strategies (lists, word webs, labeled pictures, etc.) with my students, I ask them what the term *prewriting* means. As they explain their understanding, I record their definition on chart paper. This is their definition of *prewriting*:

Prewriting is writing lots of words about a topic to brainstorm ideas. You can make lists and word webs. You can draw a picture and label it.

I tape their definitions in a highly-visible spot in the classroom. We follow defining the stage of prewriting with definitions for *drafting, revising, editing,* and *publishing.* Since I explicitly teach each step and students are involved in describing what they learned, I can feel confident that my students understand the writing process.

My Spin on Writing Workshop: A Snapshot

Although every teacher runs writing workshop in a unique way, there are fundamentals that all successful workshops incorporate. A focus lesson or mini lesson, which usually includes teacher modeling, is followed up with an opportunity for students to practice. The teacher meets with small groups and conferences with individuals. Ongoing assessment and goal setting occurs throughout the session. Gradually releasing the students from teacher instruction leads them to true mastery of a concept.

My mini lessons anchored in mentor text fit neatly into this model. In writing workshop, as a group we focus on particular narrative elements or literary devices. I allow ample time for students to discuss and formulate their definitions and understandings key concepts and techniques. When we're following up the mini lesson with writing, I ask students to apply what they've been learning about from the mentor author. I encourage them to revisit the mentor texts and our "lessons-learned" blurbs. As the writing continues, I circulate around the room to monitor understanding and confer with individual students. As needed, we stop and discuss challenges and ideas for moving forward in the writing process.

The Writer's Notebook

Another component of a successful literary environment is a place to note writing ideas and record learning experiences. My students keep a Writer's Notebook, similar to a writing scrapbook. The notebook provides a framework for introducing authors as mentors for writing. In time, this notebook becomes a treasured resource for writing.

The Writer's Notebook is where students document their writing process. It is where students record excerpts of mentor text, quoting exact passages that teach them a specific writing technique. For example, after writing and illustrating examples of personification, students might be asked to describe how the mentor text helped them learn the about that craft.

An entry about the mentor author Jonathan London and his use of personification may read something like this:

Jonathan London taught me how words can make nonliving things seem like they're living. A fire doesn't really roar like a lion or snap like a person. I wrote the leaves danced in the wind. Leaves don't really dance, but sometimes it looks like they do.

Signed Books by Student Authors

At the end of the year, my students invite their families to a book signing party. A year of learning from mentor authors can yield a cornucopia of original writings in many formats; nonfiction books, fairy tales, letters, class books, poetry books, writer's notebooks, and so on. The event is a hit with the students and their families. Young authors share the writing they have modeled after mentors such as Eric Carle, Tomie dePaola, and Gail Gibbons. At the event and beyond, students are proud to show off their efforts to their families and, more important, consider themselves authors.

Here are some suggestions for kicking off a memorable book-signing event:

- ✶ Secure a large space for the event. (We reserve the school library.)
- ✶ Ask students to make and distribute party invitations to the principal, reading teacher, librarians, and other staff. (Their attendance will be a boon, especially if on the big night some family members of students have other obligations and are unable to attend.)
- ✶ Have student volunteers make posters detailing the steps of the writing process, including how the Writer's Notebook is used to improve specific writing skills. Attach student samples.
- ✶ Days before the event, explain that authors typically write their signature on the title page of published works. (Encourage students to practice signing their names in cursive.)
- ✶ On the big day, display each student's work along with his or her Writer's Notebook. Set chairs nearby the display to invite conversation between student authors and party attendees interested reading and learning about published works.

> *"Talking about good writing is often not as powerful as immersing oneself in it. Some of the most successful mini lessons center on reading and celebrating good literature."*
>
> –Lucy Calkins

Using This Book

In the course of my teaching and writing this book, I researched clear examples of good writing techniques. The pages that follow include information about 20 mentor authors who have written texts that model critical narrative elements or literary devices.

The first section on each mentor includes background information about what inspires the author. It also offers insights on his or her particular writing process.

Each book included in the Recommended Reading list was written by the featured mentor author. Of course, if you have your own favorite texts by this author that address the writing topic you're studying, by all means use those texts.

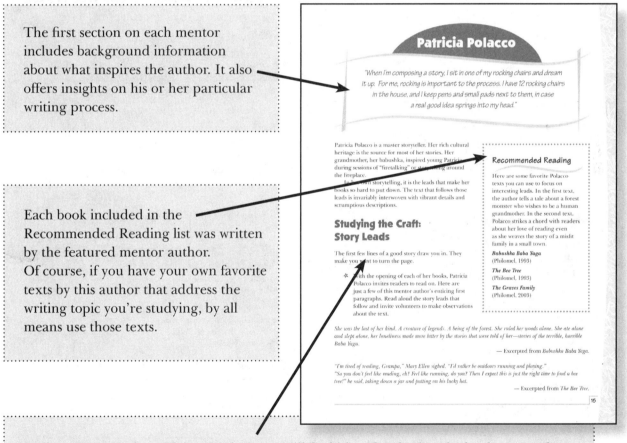

In the section on the craft in question, you will find ideas for sharing the book as a read aloud. The first time a child hears the mentor text, the experience should be for enjoyment only. Read a story to the end without stopping to discuss text features. The next reading, during the mini lesson, is where the class can focus on writer's craft.

You'll also find suggestions for setting the stage for introducing a particular narrative element or literary device.

Within the inset (page 16):

No one saw them slide into Union City that dark and dreary night. Doug and Shalleaux Graves arrived with their family of five children to take up residence in the old house on Park Street. The town clock struck wildly and ran backwards, and the water in the fountain in the village square turned crimson as their car drove by.
— Excerpted from *The Graves Family*.

✤ Read aloud a variety of Patricia Polacco's books for enjoyment, including *The Graves Family* and *Babushka Baba Yaga*. (To familiarize the class with the author's work, try sharing the books over a couple of days.)

✤ At the start of each read aloud, invite volunteers to make observations about the story leads. For example, one student might notice the suspense built by the author, the way she unveils one small tidbit of information at a time to draw the reader into the action (*Babushka Baba Yaga*). Another student might notice that a story begins in the middle of the action, right smack in the middle of dialogue (*The Bee Tree*). Still another might notice that the author takes on the role of the omniscient narrator and confidante, telling the reader about events that happen under cover of darkness (*The Graves Family*). (See the Dynamic Mini Lesson.)

Cultivating the Writer's Notebook

Set up a Patricia Polacco author center where students can examine first paragraphs to identify good leads. The center may include the following materials:
☺ a collection of Polacco's books, including *Babushka Baba Yaga* and *The Graves Family*
☺ text finders to frame the first paragraphs (Large magnifying glasses work well.)
☺ extra copies of Hooking the Reader (page 18)

✤ Distribute a copy of Hooking the Reader (page 18) to each student. Ask students to note their favorite lead from one of the Polacco books on the top of their page. Invite students to use text finders or magnifying glasses to locate the lead paragraph of the book.

✤ Students should think about why that lead appeals to them and how they can apply it to their own writing. Explain that students will find a story in their Writer's Notebook that they want to polish or may begin a new story using a story lead.

Standards Addressed
(McREL Language Arts Benchmarks Level I K–2)

✓ Drafting and Revising: Uses strategies to draft and revise written work (e.g., rereads; rearranges words, sentences, and paragraphs to improve or clarify meaning; varies sentence type; adds descriptive words and details; deletes extraneous information; incorporates suggestions from peers and teachers; sharpens the focus). (Language Arts Standard 1: benchmark 2)

16

The reading and writing activities and mini lessons in this book are standards-based.

I have turned to the recommendations of the Midcontinent Research for Education and Learning (http://www.mcrel.org) and its standards for Kindergarten through 5th grade. Most of McREL's recommendations would probably fit comfortably into most regional and state standards. As you do your lesson planning, bear in mind your state's standards and recommendations for writing. Also consider turning to professional organizations such as the International Reading Association (http://www.reading.org) and the National Council of Teachers of English (http://www.ncte.org). They offer an all-encompassing list of standards for all students engaged in language learning.

The meat, or the independent writing component, is found in the Writer's Notebook section where students apply what they've been learning. To help you with instruction, you'll be directed to one or more reproducible pages (see below) that complement your lesson plans. To get started, make photocopies of the reproducible for your students. Go over the page with them, outlining the directions and your expectations of them as developing writers. When they have completed their work, have students gather their work into their Writer's Notebook for future reference. The idea is that the Writer's Notebook is concurrently a collection of writing topics, a study in applying key skills and concepts, and a resource students can turn to again and again for inspiration and support. Below is an example of a reproducible.

Within the reproducible (page 18):

Skill Area: Story Leads

Name: _____   Date: _____

Hooking the Reader

Authors like Patricia Polacco use leads to lure readers into reading more of a story. They include clues in the lead that give the reader hints about what might happen. These clues hook the reader.

Select a lead to use as inspiration.
Which text is it from? _____
Who is the author? _____

Use the lead as a model for writing a lead of your own. It can be a lead for a story you're revising or a story you'd like to write.

_____
_____
_____
_____
_____
_____

Ask a classmate to read your lead and check a box to show how he or she feels about reading further.

Classmate's Name: _____

Are you interested in reading the story? ❑ Yes ❑ No
✤ If your classmate checked *Yes*, write the rest of the story.
✤ If your classmate checked *No*, rewrite your lead to make it more interesting. On the back of this page, write your revised lead.

URLs for Web sites of interest, suggestions for books about the author and related places to visit, as well as recommendations for professional books are included in the Other Resources section.

Other Resources

✫ Visit Patricia Polacco's Web site: **www.patriciapolacco.com**

✫ Read or view the Reading Rockets video interview: **www.readingrockets.org/books/interviews/polacco**

✫ Find ideas in *Teaching With Favorite Patricia Polacco Books* by I. A. Rhodes (Scholastic, 2002).

✫ View the video *Dream Keeper*, a visit with Patricia Polacco in her studio (Philomel, 1996).

✫ Read Polacco's autobiography *Firetalking* (Owen, 1990).

✔ Editing and Publishing: Uses strategies to edit and publish written work (e.g., proofreads using a dictionary and other resources; edits for grammar, punctuation, capitalization, and spelling at a developmentally appropriate level; incorporates illustrations or photos; uses available, appropriate technology to publish work; uses legible handwriting; shares finished products). (Language Arts Standard 1: benchmark 3)

✔ Writes for different purposes. (Language Arts Standard 1: benchmark 8)

Dynamic Mini Lesson: **Writing Story Leads**

Groeneweg copies the first paragraph of The Graves Family *on chart paper.*
Groeneweg reads the lead aloud to the class.

Groeneweg: What do you think will happen in this story?

Students give a variety of answers.

Groeneweg: Would you like to hear the rest of the story? Why or why not?

Groeneweg circles phrases, words, and ideas of interest on the chart paper.
Groeneweg reads the rest of the story.

Groeneweg: How did the lead give us clues to what was going to happen? They let us make some predictions.

Groeneweg uses a highlighter to mark the clues students mention.
If the students need more practice, Groeneweg repeats the process with Babushka Baba Yaga.

Groeneweg: Now you're going to write your own lead to a story. Remember, you want to make your readers want to read the story and give them clues to what happens.

Before you write your lead, think about the Patricia Polacco books we've read. Which book had you hooked the moment we began reading? Use that lead to encourage you when you write your own leads.

Groeneweg distributes a copy of Hooking the Reader (page18) to each student.
Students work independently on their leads and then trade papers with a classmate.
Groeneweg invites volunteers to read and discuss their leads aloud.

17

The Dynamic Mini Lesson is the explicit instruction component, the part of the lesson where students focus their attention on specific narrative elements or literary devices. Details on how to use and mark the mentor text are presented with the text itself and oftentimes by the recording of words and phrases on chart paper.

A key part of the mini lessons in my classroom is the interplay between students—the dynamic forum of discussion. Student observations and responses about mentor text give me a window into their level of understanding. Moreover, it helps students demonstrate their grasp of the use for (and ultimately, the application of) the writing technique that the mentor author exemplifies.

Lois Ehlert

"I guess everyone is influenced by his or her own experiences."

Lois Ehlert writes about things she knows. She writes from the heart: A squirrel that had squeezed through a hole in one of Ehlert's screened windows sparked the idea for *Nuts to You*. A tribute to her parents, *Hands* reflects the creative encouragement young Lois received from her mother and father.

When planning a book, Ehlert uses list-making and other prewriting strategies to energize her thinking, including reflecting on her own life to find memorable moments. In the classroom, as we turn to her texts for insight into prewriting strategies, we'll be reminded that not only are her stories often funny and relatable, but her colorful collages also bid children to dive headlong into them.

Studying the Craft: Prewriting Strategies

Finding topics to write about is challenging for some children. Before I introduced students to Lois Ehlert's methods of prewriting, I often heard choruses of the dreaded question, "What should I write about?"

✫ Read aloud a variety of Lois Ehlert's books for enjoyment. (To familiarize the class with the author's work, try sharing the books over a couple of days.)

✫ Introduce the concept of prewriting strategies. Read aloud *Under My Nose*. (See the Recommended Reading list.) Distribute a copy of Collecting Writing Ideas (page 14) to each student and invite them to brainstorm and list their own adventures and situations that seem conducive to storytelling. (See Dynamic Mini Lessons 1 and 2.)

Recommended Reading

In these favorite Ehlert texts, the author regales the reader with stories about everything from the antics of her sister's cat to building snowmen as a child. Included on this list is Ehlert's autobiography *Under My Nose*.

Feathers for Lunch
(Harcourt Brace Jovanovich, 1990)

Hands
(Harcourt Brace, 1997)

Nuts to You
(Harcourt Brace Jovanovich, 1993)

Red Leaf, Yellow Leaf
(Harcourt Brace Jovanovich, 1991)

Snowballs
(Harcourt Brace, 1995)

Top Cat
(Harcourt Brace, 1998)

Under My Nose
(Richard C. Owen, 1996)

Cultivating the Writer's Notebook

Set up a Lois Ehlert author center where students can create their own books with illustrations inspired by the mentor author.

Include the following materials:
- a collection of Ehlert's books, including *Under My Nose*
- notepads for prewriting lists
- colorful paper, origami paper, textured paper, scrapbook supplies, and odds and ends for collages
- copy paper, lined paper, stapler for book pages

☆ Have students choose one idea from their Collecting Writing Ideas sheet, then list words describing that idea and use the list to draft a story. (See *Under My Nose*, page 23.) Children can use the supplies in the Ehlert author center to publish their story with collage-style illustrations. Display the published works in the author center.

Other Resources

☆ View Reading Rockets video interview with Lois Ehlert at **www.readingrockets.org/books/interviews/ehlert**

☆ Read this interview with one of her publishers: **www.harcourtbooks.com/authorinterviews/BookInterview_Ehlert_C.asp**

Standards Addressed (McREL Benchmarks Level I K–2)

✔ Uses prewriting strategies to plan written work (Language Arts Standard 1: benchmark 1).

✔ Writes for different purposes (Language Arts Standard 1: benchmark 8).

✔ Uses writing and other methods to describe familiar persons, places, objects, or experiences (Language Arts Standard 1: benchmark 6).

Dynamic Mini Lesson 1: Collecting Writing Ideas

Groeneweg: We've read a few of Lois Ehlert's books. Let's name some . . . .

Hiroko: *Feathers for Lunch*

Jake: *Hands*

Marie: *Snowballs*

Groeneweg: Let's take a close look at *Hands*.

Groeneweg rereads Hands.

Groeneweg: Where do you think author Ehlert got the idea to write the book?

Groeneweg revisits text and elicits responses from students.

Jake: Maybe her mom and dad really did these things.

Groeneweg: Today we are going to learn how our mentor author, Lois Ehlert, comes up with ideas for her writing. Then we are going to make our own lists of ideas using her strategies.

Groeneweg: Let's read a little from Ehlert's autobiography. What does she say about finding ideas for writing?

Groeneweg reads excerpts from Under My Nose *(pages 16–20).*

Groeneweg: Where does Ehlert get her ideas for writing?

Groeneweg elicits responses like the one below and records them on chart paper. The chart is organized in the same way as the Collecting Writing Ideas reproducible. (See page 14.)

Hiroko: She writes about things that really happened to her.

Groeneweg: Now we're going to be like Lois Ehlert and collect some ideas that we as a class have done. Let's think of some things that have really happened to us.

Groeneweg gives one or two examples, such as a class trip, a recent fire drill, or getting a class pet.

Groeneweg: Now it's your turn. Think about some things that really happened to you. They can be funny events like the ones in *Top Cat* or more serious like those in *Hands*.

A few students share some of their stories.

Groeneweg: Now you're going to record some of these ideas on your Collecting Writing Ideas page.

Groeneweg hands out a copy of Collecting Writing Ideas (page 14) to each student.

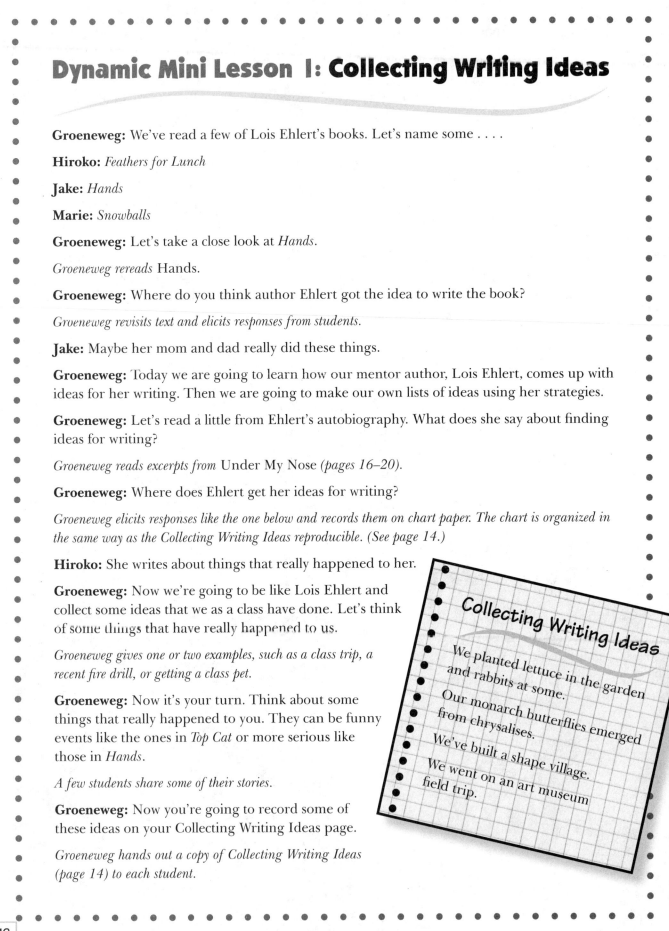

Collecting Writing Ideas

We planted lettuce in the garden and rabbits at some.

Our monarch butterflies emerged from chrysalises.

We've built a shape village.

We went on an art museum field trip.

Dynamic Mini Lesson 2: Lists for Prewriting

Groeneweg: We're going to find out how our writing mentor, Lois Ehlert, brainstorms ideas before she begins writing. To do that, we'll read some of her autobiography, *Under My Nose*.

Groeneweg reads excerpts from Under My Nose *(pages 22–23).*

Groeneweg: What does she do?

Sam: She makes lists.

Groeneweg: We're going to choose one idea from our Collecting Writing Ideas chart and make a list of words about the topic in our Writer's Notebooks.

Students vote on which idea to use. Groeneweg writes "Our Shape Village" on the top of the chart paper. Students brainstorm words about the topic and list them on chart paper.

Groeneweg: Now you're going to use your Writer's Notebook. Find where you attached the Collecting Writing Ideas page that you filled in. It's time to choose one of the ideas and write a list of words about that topic on a fresh sheet of paper in your notebook. Brainstorm any and all thoughts you have about it. Refer to the page later when you're looking for an idea.

Name: _____   Date: _____

Collecting Writing Ideas

Write words and draw pictures in each category. Write the first ideas that come to your head.

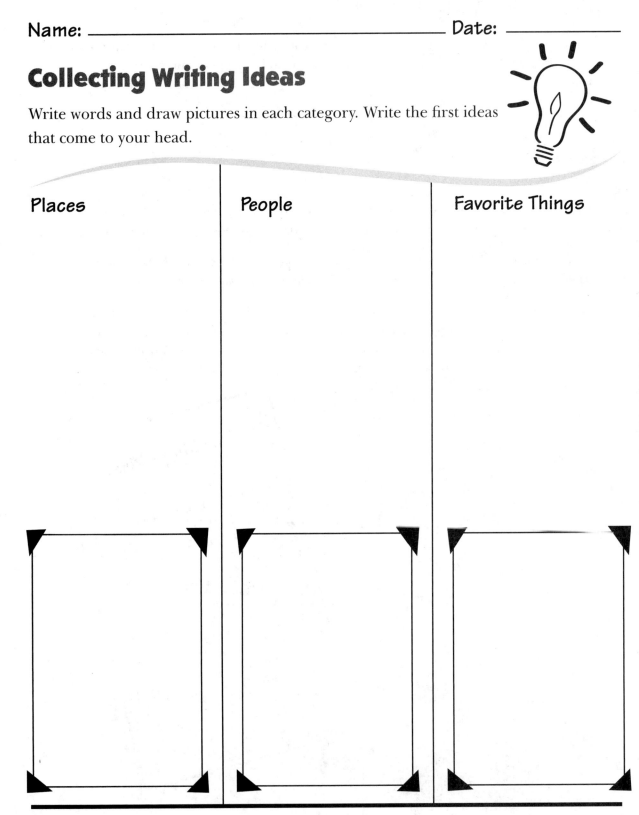

Places	People	Favorite Things

Patricia Polacco

"When I'm composing a story, I sit in one of my rocking chairs and dream it up. For me, rocking is important to the process. I have 12 rocking chairs in the house, and I keep pens and small pads next to them, in case a real good idea springs into my head."

Patricia Polacco is a master storyteller. Her rich cultural heritage is the source for most of her stories. Her grandmother, her babushka, inspired young Patricia during sessions of "firetalking" or storytelling around the fireplace.

In her own storytelling, it is the leads that make her books so hard to put down. The text that follows those leads is invariably interwoven with vibrant details and scrumptious descriptions.

Studying the Craft: Story Leads

The first few lines of a good story draw you in. They make you want to turn the page.

✿ With the opening of each of her books, Patricia Polacco invites readers to read on. Here are just a few of this mentor author's enticing first paragraphs. Read aloud the story leads that follow and invite volunteers to make observations about the text.

Recommended Reading

Here are some favorite Polacco texts you can use to focus on interesting leads. In the first text, the author tells a tale about a forest monster who wishes to be a human grandmother. In the second text, Polacco strikes a chord with readers about her love of reading even as she weaves the story of a misfit family in a small town.

Babushka Baba Yaga
(Philomel, 1993)

The Bee Tree
(Philomel, 1993)

The Graves Family
(Philomel, 2003)

She was the last of her kind. A creature of legends. A being of the forest. She ruled her woods alone. She ate alone and slept alone, her loneliness made more bitter by the stories that were told of her—stories of the terrible, horrible Baba Yaga.

— Excerpted from *Babushka Baba Yaga.*

"I'm tired of reading, Grampa," Mary Ellen sighed. "I'd rather be outdoors running and playing."
"So you don't feel like reading, eh? Feel like running, do you? Then I expect this is just the right time to find a bee tree!" he said, taking down a jar and putting on his lucky hat.

— Excerpted from *The Bee Tree.*

No one saw them slide into Union City that dark and dreary night. Doug and Shalleaux Graves arrived with their family of five children to take up residence in the old house on Park Street. The town clock struck wildly and ran backwards, and the water in the fountain in the village square turned crimson as their car drove by.

— Excerpted from *The Graves Family.*

✰ Read aloud a variety of Patricia Polacco's books for enjoyment, including *The Graves Family* and *Babushka Baba Yaga.* (To familiarize the class with the author's work, try sharing the books over a couple of days.)

✰ At the start of each read aloud, invite volunteers to make observations about the story leads. For example, one student might notice the suspense built by the author, the way she unveils one small tidbit of information at a time to draw the reader into the action (*Babushka Baba Yaga.*). Another student might notice that a story begins in the middle of the action, right smack in the middle of dialogue (*The Bee Tree*). Still another might notice that the author takes on the role of the omniscient narrator and confidante, telling the reader about events that happen under cover of darkness (*The Graves Family*). (See the Dynamic Mini Lesson.)

Cultivating the Writer's Notebook

Set up a Patricia Polacco author center where students can examine first paragraphs to identify good leads. The center may include the following materials:

◎ a collection of Polacco's books, including *Babushka Baba Yaga* and *The Graves Family*

◎ text finders to frame the first paragraphs (Large magnifying glasses work well.)

◎ extra copies of Hooking the Reader (page 18)

✰ Distribute a copy of Hooking the Reader (page 18) to each student. Ask students to note their favorite lead from one of the Polacco books on the top of their page. Invite students to use text finders or magnifying glasses to locate the lead paragraph of the book.

✰ Students should think about why that lead appeals to them and how they can apply it to their own writing. Explain that students will find a story in their Writer's Notebook that they want to polish or may begin a new story using a story lead.

Standards Addressed (McREL Language Arts Benchmarks Level I K–2)

✔ Drafting and Revising: Uses strategies to draft and revise written work (e.g., rereads; rearranges words, sentences, and paragraphs to improve or clarify meaning; varies sentence type; adds descriptive words and details; deletes extraneous information; incorporates suggestions from peers and teachers; sharpens the focus). (Language Arts Standard 1: benchmark 2)

Other Resources

✿ Visit Patricia Polacco's Web site: **www.patriciapolacco.com**

✿ Read or view the Reading Rockets video interview: **www.readingrockets.org/books/interviews/polacco**

✿ Find ideas in *Teaching With Favorite Patricia Polacco Books* by I. A. Rhodes (Scholastic, 2002).

✿ View the video *Dream Keeper*, a visit with Patricia Polacco in her studio (Philomel, 1996).

✿ Read Polacco's autobiography *Firetalking* (Owen, 1990).

✔ Editing and Publishing: Uses strategies to edit and publish written work (e.g., proofreads using a dictionary and other resources; edits for grammar, punctuation, capitalization, and spelling at a developmentally appropriate level; incorporates illustrations or photos; uses available, appropriate technology to publish work; uses legible handwriting; shares finished products). (Language Arts Standard 1: benchmark 3)

✔ Writes for different purposes. (Language Arts Standard 1: benchmark 8)

Dynamic Mini Lesson: Writing Story Leads

Groeneweg copies the first paragraph of The Graves Family *on chart paper.*
Groeneweg reads the lead aloud to the class.

Groeneweg: What do you think will happen in this story?

Students give a variety of answers.

Groeneweg: Would you like to hear the rest of the story? Why or why not?

Groeneweg circles phrases, words, and ideas of interest on the chart paper.
Groeneweg reads the rest of the story.

Groeneweg: How did the lead give us clues to what was going to happen?
They let us make some predictions.

Groeneweg uses a highlighter to mark the clues students mention.
If the students need more practice, Groeneweg repeats the process with Babushka Baba Yaga.

Groeneweg: Now you're going to write your own lead to a story. Remember, you want to make your readers want to read the story and give them clues to what happens.

Before you write your lead, think about the Patricia Polacco books we've read. Which book had you hooked the moment we began reading? Use that lead to encourage you when you write your own leads.

Groeneweg distributes a copy of Hooking the Reader *(page 18) to each student.*
Students work independently on their leads and then trade papers with a classmate.
Groeneweg invites volunteers to read and discuss their leads aloud.

Name: _____ Date: _____

Hooking the Reader

Authors like Patricia Polacco use leads to lure readers into reading more of a story. They include clues in the lead that give the reader hints about what might happen. Those clues hook the reader.

Select a lead to use as inspiration.

Which text is it from? _____

Who is the author? _____

Use the lead as a model for writing a lead of your own. It can be a lead for a story you're revising or a story you'd like to write.

_____

_____

_____

_____

_____

Ask a classmate to read your lead and check a box to show how he or she feels about reading further.

Classmate's Name: _____

Are you interested in reading the story? ❏ Yes ❏ No

✰ If your classmate checked *Yes*, write the rest of the story.

✰ If your classmate checked *No*, rewrite your lead to make it more interesting. On the back of this page, write your revised lead.

Tomi dePaola

"I do a first draft that no one sees but me. I do a lot of my writing in my head first, just thinking the story through."

If you ask primary-age children who their favorite author is, you're likely to hear Tomie dePaola's name. DePaola's accessible illustrations and his affinity for drawing hearts secure him a special place in the minds of young readers. In addition, he's the winner of a Caldecott Honor Award for *Strega Nona* and the author and illustrator of more than 200 children's books.

To write his fanciful stories dePaola often mines his own Irish and Italian background. His own grandparents served as character models for *Tom*. While we'll look at *Tom*, we'll also look closely at a few of dePaola's other books for examples of clearly defined story elements.

Recommended Reading

Tomie dePaola takes readers on whimsical journeys, from autobiographical stories that draw on events from his own childhood (*Tom*) to humorous, cautionary tales about muddling with magic (*Strega Nona*).

Stagestruck
(Putnam, 2005)

Strega Nona: An Old Tale
(Prentice-Hall, 1975)

Strega Nona Takes a Vacation
(Putnam, 2000)

Tom
(Putnam, 1993)

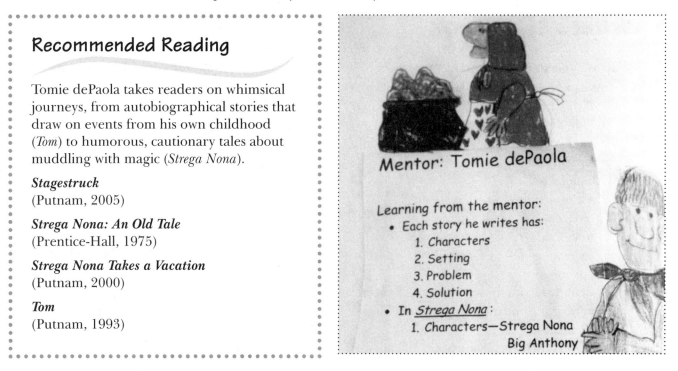

Mentor: Tomie dePaola

Learning from the mentor:
• Each story he writes has:
   1. Characters
   2. Setting
   3. Problem
   4. Solution
• In *Strega Nona*:
   1. Characters—Strega Nona
      Big Anthony

Studying the Craft: Story Elements

✵ Read aloud a variety of Tomie dePaola's books for enjoyment. (To familiarize the class with the author's work, try sharing the books over a couple of days.)

✵ Introduce the concept of story elements (characters, setting, problem, solution). Read aloud *Strega Nona* (see Recommended Reading list) then distribute a copy of Identifying Story Elements (page 23) to each child. (Use the Dynamic Mini Lesson as a guide.)

Characters

A favorite of children, *Strega Nona* is the most familiar of all of Tomie dePaola's characters. When children meet the bumbling Big Anthony, they will surely double up with laughter. From *Strega Nona* to *Tom* or *Tony's Bread*, strong characters abound, and dePaola makes it effortless for young readers to discern the main and supporting characters.

Setting

Calabria, Italy is a familiar setting for readers of Tomie dePaola's books. Students come to recognize the countryside of southern Italy after reading a few Strega Nona stories.

Problem and Solution

Even the most serious of students giggle at the overflowing pasta pot in *Strega Nona*. They love it when Strega Nona saves the day and solves Big Anthony's predicament with a creative solution. Tomie dePaola includes conflicts in his stories that invite students to problem solve even as they entertain. (See the Dynamic Mini Lesson.)

Cultivating the Writer's Notebook

Set up a Tomie dePaola author center where students can find evidence of story elements in a variety of the mentor author's books. The center may include the following materials:

- a collection of dePaola's books, including *Strega Nona*
- a metal pot
- a long-handled wooden spoon
- different types of dry pasta (Yarn works well, too.)
- a chart displaying Strega Nona's pasta pot song
- a chart that identifies the story elements in Strega Nona (See the Dynamic Mini Lesson.)
- nonfiction books that feature Italian landscapes and cityscapes
- writing paper and notepads

Other Resources

- ✪ Visit Tomie dePaola's official Web site: **www.tomie.com,** and then check out his blog: **www.tomiesblog.blogspot.com**
- ✪ Watch the Reading Rockets interview with Tomie dePaola: **www.readingrockets.org/ books/interviews/depaola**
- ✪ Read a biography, such as *Tomie dePaola: His Art and His Stories* by B. Ellman (Putnam, 1999) or *Tomie dePaola* by E. Braun (Pebble Books, 2005).
- ✪ Find lesson ideas in *Teaching With Favorite Tomie dePaola Books* by L. DeAngelis and R. Callan (Scholastic, 2004).
- ✪ Invite independent readers to read dePaola's autobiographical chapter books, a series that begins with *26 Fairmount Avenue* (Putnam, 1999).

✪ Distribute a copy of Identifying Story Elements (page 23) to each student. Explain that students should use the supplies in the Tomie dePaola center to plan their own stories that include key story elements (characters, setting, problem, solution).

✪ When students are ready, have them write, edit, and then publish their own books. Students who include pasta in their stories may embellish their book covers with glued-on pasta or yarn. Display all of the published books in the author center.

Standards Addressed
(McREL Benchmarks Level I K–2)

✔ Uses prewriting strategies to plan written work (Language Arts Standards 1: benchmark 1).

✔ Writes for different purposes (Language Arts Standards 1: benchmark 8).

✔ Uses writing and other methods to describe familiar persons, places, objects, or experiences (Language Arts Standards 1: benchmark 6).

Dynamic Mini Lesson:
Identifying Story Elements

Groeneweg: I'm going to reread *Strega Nona* by Tomie dePaola today. I want you to listen for the story elements. We've talked about story elements. Who can remember one of them?

Groeneweg writes each element after volunteers identify them.

Groeneweg: We're going to listen for evidence of these elements while I read the story again. Put a thumb up when you hear evidence one of these elements in the story. We'll stop and record the example on our chart.

Groeneweg begins reading the story. At the end of the first page, she looks for a student with his or her thumb up.

Groeneweg: What story element did you notice, Norma?

Norma: The setting. He wrote where the story happens.

Groeneweg: Yes. Here's the text "In a town in Calabria, a long time ago . . . ."

Groeneweg uses a sticky note to underscore the text in the book and records the excerpt under the "setting" heading of the chart.

Groeneweg: Let's continue reading and looking for more evidence.

Groeneweg continues reading the story. As she turns the pages, she looks around the group for a volunteer.

Callum: Strega Nona is a character.

Groeneweg uses a sticky note to underscore the text in the book and records the name Strega Nona *under the "character" heading of the chart.*

Groeneweg: You guys have the hang of this. Let's keep reading.

Groeneweg continues reading the story. As she turns the pages, she looks around the group for a volunteer.

Manny: Big Anthony is a character, too.

Groeneweg uses a sticky note to underscore the text in the book and records the name Big Anthony *under the "character" heading of the chart.*

Groeneweg continues reading the story. As she turns the pages, she looks around for more volunteers.

Emma: Big Anthony doesn't know about the three kisses, and he can't stop the pasta pot. That's the problem.

Groeneweg uses a sticky note to underscore the text in the book. She writes the excerpt under the "problem" heading of the chart.

Groeneweg continues reading the story. As she turns the pages, she looks for more volunteers.

Gregory: Strega Nona helps Big Anthony solve his problem. She blows the three kisses, and the pot stops cooking pasta.

Groeneweg uses a sticky note to underscore the text in the book. She writes the excerpt under the "solution" heading of the chart.

Groeneweg: Let's read our chart about story elements. What words did the author use to show us the setting?

Groeneweg and students read aloud the mentor text that describes the setting.

The lesson continues in the same manner, with students rereading the mentor text and discussing story elements.

Groeneweg: Now you're going to begin thinking about a story of your own that includes the story elements we've been learning out. I'll give you a sheet to help you organize your thoughts.

　　And don't forget to use the Tomie dePaola center for ideas and quick access to the mentor text we've been looking at today. For reference, I'll post this chart we've made in the center, too.

Groeneweg hands out a copy of Identifying Story Elements *(page 23) to each student. After completing the sheet, students begin the process of writing the story.*

Name: _____ Date: _____

Identifying Story Elements

Characters
Main Character
Other Characters

Setting
Where
When

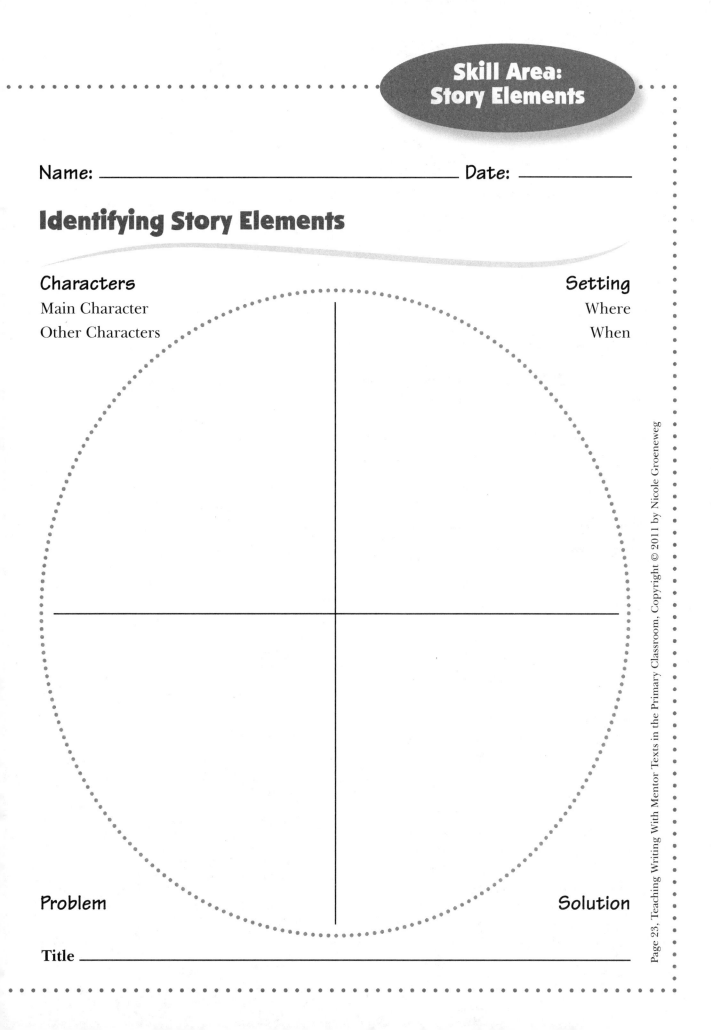

Problem

Solution

Title _____

Eric Carle

"Let's put it this way: if you are a novelist, I think you start out with a 20 word idea, and you work at it and you wind up with a 200,000 word novel. We, picture-book people, or at least I, start out with 200,000 words and I reduce it to 20."

Now world-renowned for his distinctive picture books, Carle's first dabble into children's books was as an illustrator for Bill Martin Jr.'s *Brown Bear, Brown Bear What Do You See?* (Holt, Rhinehart and Winston, 1967) Before long, Carle began writing his own stories accompanied by illustrations. One of these early forays into writing was a story about a week in the life of a worm named Willy. That story evolved into a more familiar one, *The Very Hungry Caterpillar*.

Many of Carle's stories serve as valuable mentor texts on story sequencing techniques. In some books, the reader encounters different animals or objects in an order that propels the plot action forward. Other stories depict life cycles of insects or plants. And within one story, attentive readers may find multiple sequencing techniques interwoven.

Studying the Craft: Sequence of Events

Children love to retell Eric Carle's stories. Clearly defined sequences make it easy for them.

✰ Read aloud a variety of Eric Carle books for enjoyment. Ask the children to concentrate on listening for clues about story sequence. Ask: *What hints does the author give us that the story is moving from beginning to end?* (To familiarize the class with the author's work, try sharing the books over a couple of days.)

✰ Explain that, like other authors, mentor author Eric Carle matches the sequence for his story with the purpose for his writing. Tell the group that you will be reading aloud a text by Eric Carle and that they should listen for evidence of the type of sequence he uses for that story. (On page 25, you'll find suggestions for pairing read aloud stories with the type of sequencing they best illustrate.).

Recommended Reading

Spotlight how story sequence moves a story along with any of these beloved Carle texts. Invite students to explore numerical sequence, chronological time, and life cycle as organizational tools for story writing.

The Grouchy Ladybug
(Crowell, 1977)

The Tiny Seed
(Crowell, 1970)

The Very Busy Spider
(Philomel, 1984)

The Very Clumsy Click Beetle
(Philomel, 1999)

The Very Hungry Caterpillar
(Collins, 1969)

The Very Lonely Firefly
(Philomel, 1995)

The Very Quiet Cricket
(Philomel, 1990)

* After reading the selected story aloud, discuss what happened in the story. Explain that an author who writes narrative or nonfiction pieces can turn to the sequencing of events as way of organizing their writing, helping a reader learn what happens when. When students are ready, distribute a copy of Chronological Time (pages 29 and 30) to each student. (See the Dynamic Mini Lesson as a guide.)

The sequences tackled by this mentor author include numerical sequence (first, second, third), chronological (hours, days, weeks), and life cycle (relating to animals, plants, and insects).

Numerical Sequence

Introduce the concept of story sequence by asking students to tell you about what has happened in their day so far. After a few students have told the class what happened first, second, and third, explain that organizing a story around time can be a useful technique for an author to move the action forward.

* In *The Very Hungry Caterpillar* the caterpillar first ate **one** apple, then **two** pears, then **three** plums, then **four** strawberries, and finally **five** oranges.

* In *The Very Lonely Firefly,* the young firefly encounters different light sources that he believes to be other fireflies. **First** he sees a light bulb. **Second** he comes across a candle. A flashlight becomes his **third** glowing light. The story continues until he finally stumbles upon other fireflies.

Chronological Time

In each of the insect books, Eric Carle arranges the sequence in a different time schedule. A clock guides the Grouchy Ladybug through the day. At each hour the cantankerous ladybug meets a new animal.

* The very hungry caterpillar eats his way through a week's worth of days and then forms a chrysalis. Within a few weeks, the tiny caterpillar hatches from an egg and grows into a butterfly.

* Over a two day period, the beetle in *The Very Clumsy Click Beetle* learns to flip away from danger. In this story, Eric Carle uses "timely" words and phrases to indicate the progression of time (at noon, in the afternoon, in the evening, tomorrow).

* In *The Very Quiet Cricket,* time is signified by different greetings. Diurnal insects such as the praying mantis addressed the cricket with "Hello" or "Good Morning." The mosquitoes, which are nocturnal insects, greeted the cricket with "Good Night!"

* The spider in *The Very Busy Spider,* while not an insect, fits into Eric Carle's sequencing pattern for the insect book series. The story starts as the spider begins to spin her web "early one morning" and concludes with the exhausted spider sleeping at night. Note: A newer version of this story includes a hands-on clock to show time progression through the busy day.

Life Cycles

Some of Eric Carle's insect stories have more than one layer of sequence, weaving life cycles into the numeric sequencing of the story. In fact, the problems in the story are resolved when certain stages of the life cycle come to fruition.

✧ The cricket in *The Very Quiet Cricket* hatches from an egg and grows until he is in his adult stage and no longer silent.

✧ In *The Very Hungry Caterpillar*, the caterpillar hatches from an egg, eats his way through the larva stage, uses the stored food during the pupa stage, and then transforms into a butterfly.

Cultivating the Writer's Notebook

Set up an Eric Carle writing center, a Very Insecty area, where students can create their own books inspired by the mentor author. (Links to science concepts will be made through observation of insects. Links to math concepts will be made using calendars and clocks.) This center may include the following materials:

◉ a collection of Eric Carle's insect books
◉ a collection of nonfiction insect books
◉ analog clocks for students to manipulate time sequences
◉ clock or circle-shaped stamps to add clock faces to student-made stories
◉ calendars for students to see day and month sequences
◉ a collection of insect exoskeletons or nests to use as models for illustrations
◉ insect puppets for acting out stories
◉ copy paper, lined paper, stapler for assembling book pages
◉ color tissue paper, patterned craft paper, scissors, and glue (for making collages)
◉ crayons, watercolor paints, and water in a container (for painting and gluing)

✧ Tell students that they will use a planning sheet to organize their own "Very... Insect." books using chronological sequence. When students are ready, distribute a copy of the Chronological Time sheets (pages 29 and 30) to each student. After completing the graphic organizers, have students attach the pages to their Writer's Notebooks and begin the process of writing the story.

✧ When students are ready to publish their work, have them use the supplies in the writing center to publish their story with collages reminiscent of Eric Carle's. To complete their book covers, students can arrange pictures with small pieces of tissue paper and glue. Next, students glaze the tissue paper with water-thinned glue to create a smooth and shiny effect (over the tissue paper area only). Finally, students can use a wax-resist method with crayons to add details to the rest of the cover.

Standards Addressed (McREL Benchmarks Level I K–2)

✔ Uses strategies to organize written work (e.g., includes a beginning, middle, and ending; uses a sequence of events). (Language Arts Standard 1: benchmark 5)

✔ Writes in a variety of forms or genres (e.g., picture books, friendly letters, stories, poems, information pieces, invitations, personal experience narratives, messages, responses to literature). (Language Arts Standard 1: benchmark 7)

Other Resources

✧ Visit The Eric Carle Museum of Picture Book Art in Amherst, Massachusetts. Check out Eric Carle's Web site: **www.eric-carle.com**

✧ Watch the Reading Rockets video interview with Eric Carle: **www.readingrockets.org/books/interviews/carle**

✧ Borrow and watch the DVD of *The Very Hungry Caterpillar* from a local library.

✧ Read an autobiography and retrospective of Carle's art, *The Art of Eric Carle* (Philomel, 1996).

Dynamic Mini Lesson: Chronological Sequence

Groeneweg holds up the big book version of The Very Hungry Caterpillar *to show students.*

Groeneweg: I'm going to reread *The Very Hungry Caterpillar*. While you're listening, I want you to put your thumbs up when you hear a word or group of words that are clues to when an event is happening.

Groeneweg begins reading the story. At the end of the first page, she looks for a volunteer with his or her thumb up.

Yuki: Well, Eric Carle wrote, "He was born on Saturday."

Groeneweg: Yes. Here's the text.

Groeneweg uses a sticky note to underscore the text in the book with the word Saturday.

Ethan: There's the sentence, "He ate an apple on Monday and two pears on Tuesday."

Groeneweg uses a sticky note to underscore the words Monday *and* Tuesday.

Groeneweg and students continue in this matter through the entire book.

Groeneweg: Now we're going to view the events in the story on a wall calendar. When we get to text we've marked, we'll write what happens on a sticky note and attach it to the calendar.

Groeneweg reads to the page where the caterpillar emerges from the egg.

Groeneweg: Here's what we need for the calendar. Yuki, will you place it for us?

On Saturday a very tiny caterpillar popped out of an egg.

Yuki places the sticky note on the "Saturday" spot of the calendar.

Groeneweg turns the page to show underscored text. She asks students to dictate while she writes the note for the calendar. She continues in this manner until the book is finished and the calendar is complete.

He ate a green leaf on Sunday, but he was still hungry.

Groeneweg: Let's look at how Eric Carle used time to order the events of the book.

Groeneweg points to the calendar.

Groeneweg: This mentor author uses days of the week to show us when things happen in the story. He uses what's called the story sequence. In fact, let's take time now for recording what we've learned about time words in your Writer's Notebooks.

On Monday he ate one apple.

Groeneweg: Now you're going to begin thinking about writing a story of your own, one that like *The Very Hungry Caterpillar* follows a chronological time sequence. In a moment, I'll give you a sheet to help you organize your ideas.

As you're going through the writing process, please use the Eric Carle center. I've included mentor texts and a lot of other materials to get you started. For reference, I'll post our calendar in the center, too.

Groeneweg distributes a copy of Chronological Time (pages 29 and 30) to each student. After completing the pages, students begin the process of writing a story.

Name: _____ Date: _____

Chronological Time

Story Title

Beginning

Middle

Ending

Make a list of events in your story. Draw pictures to show what happens during each event.

Event 1. _____

_____

_____

_____

Event 2. _____

_____

_____

_____

Event 3. _____

_____

_____

_____

Event 4. _____

_____

_____

_____

Event 5. _____

_____

_____

_____

Jan Brett

"I draw borders when I have too many ideas. In The Mitten, the borders show Nicki trekking through the woods and scaring different animals out of their hiding places. When you turn a page in the book, you can see the animal that comes next."

Author and illustrator Jan Brett researches her subjects thoroughly. Consequently, she is able to include authentic details in all her stories as well as the beautiful images that accompany them. Plus, traveling to diverse locations helps Jan discover interesting, unique elements.

Recommended Reading

Here are some texts you can use to focus on foreshadowing and on how Jan Brett accomplishes it.

Armadillo Rodeo
(Putnam, 1995)

Daisy Comes Home
(Putnam, 2002)

The Hat
(Putnam, 1997)

The Mitten: A Ukrainian Folktale
(Putnam, 1989)

The Three Little Dassies
(Putnam, 2010)
A South African retelling of
The Three Little Pigs

The Umbrella
(Putnam, 2004)

Studying the Craft: Foreshadowing

Foreshadowing, the use of hints or clues to suggest what might come later in the story, is not often taught to young students. Jan Brett is a mentor author who demonstrates foreshadowing in a simple way, incorporating the hints within the intricate illustrations of her page borders. It's a technique that young writers can replicate with ease. Once they understand the concept of foreshadowing through a visual means, developing writers can more readily transition to including foreshadowing through writing.

✫ Introduce foreshadowing as a technique that mentor authors like Jan Brett use to invite their readers to make predictions about the text. The authors tuck clues into their writing that hint at what events might come later in the story.

✫ Read aloud a variety of Jan Brett's books for enjoyment. (To familiarize the class with the author's work, try sharing the books over a couple of days.)

Cultivating the Writer's Notebook

Set up a Jan Brett author center where students can create their own books with illustrations inspired by the author mentor. Include the following materials:

- ◎ a collection of Jan Brett's books
- ◎ a collection of nonfiction books about woodland animals to use as models for illustrations
- ◎ extra copies of the Sprinkling Clues reproducible (page 34)
- ◎ stapler, construction paper, card stock, and glue sticks for assembling published books

✯ Invite students to write their own stories that feature foreshadowing. They can use the supplies in the Jane Brett center to publish their story. Display the published works in the author center.

✯ For an extra challenge, ask students to make a book jacket for their original stories. The jacket should include clues around the border that offer readers hints at the story elements.

Other Resources

✯ Visit Jan Brett's Web site: **www.janbrett.com**

✯ View videos of Jan Brett in action: **http://www.janbrettvideos.com/ video/video_main_page.htm**

✯ Read Jan Brett's blog: **http:// www.janbrettvideos.com/video/ video_main_page.htm**

Standards Addressed (McREL Benchmarks Level I K–2)

✔ Uses prewriting strategies to plan written work (Language Arts Standard 1: benchmark 1).

✔ Drafting and Revising: Uses strategies to draft and revise written work (e.g., rereads; rearranges words, sentences, and paragraphs to improve or clarify meaning; varies sentence type; adds descriptive words and details; deletes extraneous information; incorporates suggestions from peers and teachers; sharpens the focus). (Language Arts Standard 1: benchmark 2)

✔ Editing and Publishing: Uses strategies to edit and publish written work (e.g., proofreads using a dictionary and other resources; edits for grammar, punctuation, capitalization, and spelling at a developmentally appropriate level; incorporates illustrations or photos; uses available, appropriate technology to publish work; uses legible handwriting; shares finished products). (Language Arts Standard 1: benchmark 3)

✔ Writes for different purposes (Language Arts Standard 1: benchmark 8).

✔ Uses descriptive and precise language that clarifies and enhances ideas (e.g., concrete words and phrases, common figures of speech, sensory details). (Level 3–5 Language Arts Standard 2: benchmark 1)

Dynamic Mini Lesson: Foreshadowing

Any of Jan Brett's texts work well for this mini lesson. For this lesson, Groeneweg selected The Three Dassies.

Groeneweg: Let's take a closer look at Jan Brett's *The Three Dassies*.

Groeneweg shows the cover of the book to students.

Groeneweg: While we read, I want you to look at the pictures and listen to the words. See if you can predict what will happen next.

Groeneweg begins reading the story. After a few pages, she asks students to predict what will happen next in the story.

Groeneweg: What do you think is going to happen next?

Several students respond, making observations about clues in the text. Several more students point out that there are distinct clues about what will happen in Brett's border illustrations.

Groeneweg: You've spotted her technique. Mentor author Jan Brett uses foreshadowing. She peppers her stories with images and word clues to foreshadow what will happen next in the story. Now, while I read the rest of the story, look for her hints and make some predictions. Then see if you're right.

Groeneweg continues reading to the end of the book.

Groeneweg: Okay. We've seen foreshadowing in action. As writers, you're going to create a story that offers words and images a reader can use for making predictions. Not only will using foreshadowing engage your readers with your text, it will make your writing more interesting to read.

Groeneweg shows a copy of the Sprinkling Clues reproducible (page 34) to the group.

Groeneweg: In a moment, I'll give you a sheet like this one to help you plan your story. For now, look at this page with me and notice the spaces along the borders of the page. There's space for drawing, for giving visual cues. And remember that readers like to predict and read to find out if they're right. So, try to sprinkle clues. Your readers will look for both words and pictures.

Groeneweg distributes a copy of Sprinkling Clues (page 34) to each student. Students use the sheet as templates for writing, filling the borders will illustrations and adding narrative text that offers readers some clues about what will happen next.

Name: _____ Date: _____

Sprinkling Clues

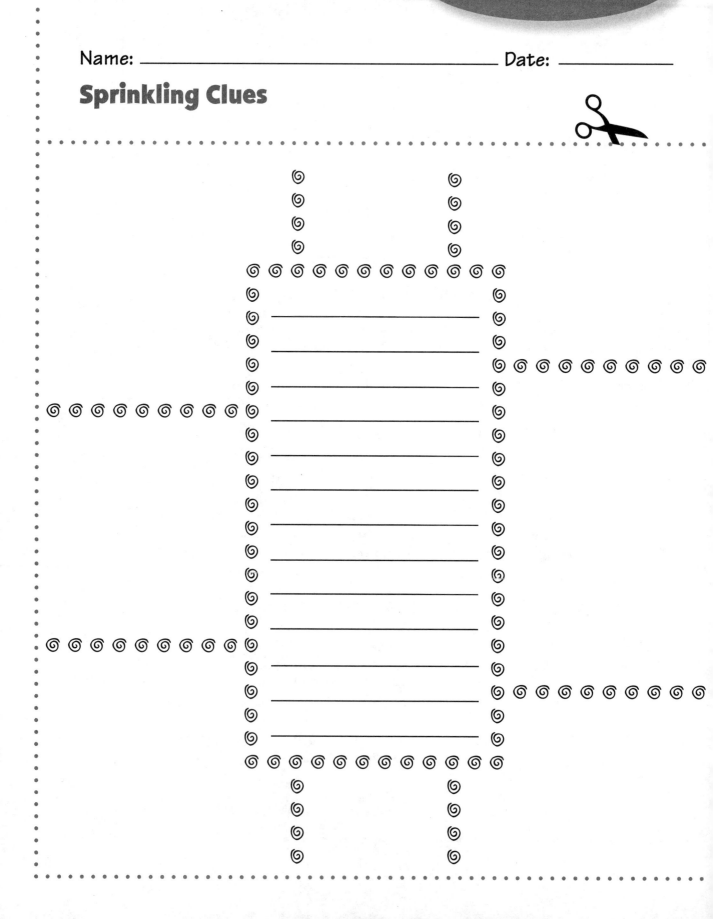

Karma Wilson

"As for how ideas come to me—I think in words, I feel in words—I see words when I create, when I speak, when I sing... visible (in my mind) written words."

Karma Wilson's love of animals and the wilderness they inhabit is evident in stories and celebrated in her rhyme-filled books. Wilson explains, "I especially love to write in rhyme because I think that well written rhyme naturally teaches children to expand their vocabulary and love books and reading."

Children also enjoy the beat or rhythm of the words in Karma Wilson's texts and find her storylines irresistible. In this book, we turn students' attention to Wilson's texts as prime examples of rhyme and rhythm.

Studying the Craft: Rhyme and Rhythm

I haven't met a child who doesn't love text that rhymes. Rhymes are fun! Plus, hearing them helps children note differences in words and strengthens developing phonemic awareness skills.

- Read aloud a variety of Karma Wilson's books for enjoyment. (To familiarize the class with the author's work, try sharing the books over a couple of days.)

- Introduce the literary device of rhyme. Read aloud *Bear Snores On*. (See the Recommended Reading list.) Invite students to identify the rhyming words each time you read a couplet. Record the list on chart paper for future reference. As a group, discuss how rhyme affects the pace of the text. How does it make us feel about reading on? Invite volunteers to offer insights about why they think Karma Wilson uses a lot of rhyme in her texts. (See the Dynamic Mini Lesson 1.)

- Introduce rhythm, a literary device authors use to pace and enliven text, among other reasons. Young readers can't help but be acquainted with rhythm in text, but often don't realize it. To begin, read aloud *Bear Wants More*. Invite students to clap the rhythm of the sentences while you read aloud. After reading, discuss how rhythm influences how we read a story. Invite volunteers to offer opinions about what they think rhythm adds to a story. (See the Dynamic Mini Lesson 2.)

Recommended Reading

Spotlight how authors use sentence patterns with any of these Wilson texts.

Bear Snores On
(Little Simon, 2005)

Bear Wants More
(McElderry Books, 2003)

A Frog in a Bog
(McElderry Books, 2003)

Cultivating the Writer's Notebook

Set up a Karma Wilson rhyme and rhythm center where students can read and write rhyming poems and stories, and then work together on a collaborative collection booklet of storybook rhymes. Include the following materials:

◉ a collection of Karma Wilson's books, including *Bear Snores On*
◉ a collection of poetry books
◉ lists of word-family words
◉ lists of rhyming words
◉ copy paper, lined paper, stapler for book pages
◉ premade blank booklets

✫ Have students choose one idea from their Collecting Writing Ideas sheet (page 14) in their Writer's Notebooks. Ask students to write a list of words and phrases that rhyme with the idea. For example, a student who selects the idea "my pet snake" might make a list of rhyming phrases that include "fluffy cake," "little Jake," and "by the lake." Students can arrange the phrases as needed to create a story. Tell students to use the supplies in the writing center to polish and publish their writing. Display the completed works in the author center. Consider naming the class's collection of stories *Rhyme Time*.

✫ To take the rhythm component of the mini lesson further, encourage students to do their writing with the same rhythm as *Bear Snores On*. For younger writers, write a story as a group. Transcribe student ideas with an overhead projector or whiteboard. Edit the writing together, keeping a careful eye on rhyme and rhythm. Then invite volunteers to record the story and illustrate it for publication.

Other Resources

✫ Visit Karma Wilson's Web site **www.karmawilson.com**

Standards Addressed (McREL Benchmarks Level I K–2)

✔ Uses prewriting strategies to plan written work (Language Arts Standard 1: benchmark 1).

✔ Writes in a variety of forms or genres (e.g., picture books, friendly letters, stories, poems, information pieces, invitations, personal experience narratives, messages, responses to literature). (Language Arts Standard 1: benchmark 7)

✔ Writes for different purposes (Language Arts Standard 1: benchmark 8).

Dynamic Mini Lesson 1: Rhyme

Groeneweg: We're going to reread *Bear Snores On*. This time we're going to listen for rhyming words.

Groeneweg reads Bear Snores On *and stops at the end of each rhyming couplet.*

Groeneweg: Are there words that rhyme? What are they?

Groeneweg records student responses on chart paper.
Groeneweg continues in this manner until the story is finished and a list of rhyming words has been generated and recorded.

Groeneweg: Now you're going to write two sentences that rhyme. You can use the words from our list or you can think of your own rhyming words. Thinking of word-family words is a good place to start.

Have students record their rhymes in their Writer's Notebooks.

Groeneweg: Begin thinking about writing a funny story of your own. The story should include rhyming words.

Groeneweg distributes a copy of Storytime Rhyme (page 38) to each student.

Dynamic Mini Lesson 2: Rhythm

Groeneweg: Today we're going to read another book by the same mentor author, Karma Wilson. This book is titled *Bear Wants More*. Let's and listen to the rhythm in the text.

Groeneweg reads the first page of the story using the rhythm.
Read the page again, but this time read it in a monotone without rhythm.

Groeneweg: Which way do you like to hear the story? Why?

Bennett: The first way you read it. It sounds better.

Ana: It's more fun to read.

Rose: It reminds me of music.

Groeneweg: Now I'll read the rest of the story. Clap along with the rhythm.

Groeneweg reads the rest of the book.
Students clap along with the rhythm of her reading.

Groeneweg: Now try talking to the classmate next to you in that same rhythm.

Students speak to each other using the same rhythm of the book.
Groeneweg allows several minutes for students to practice.

Name: _____ Date: _____

Storytime Rhyme

Topic or Main Character's Name _____
_____

Story Title (Make it rhyme!)_____
_____
_____

What are some words that rhyme with the topic or main character's name? (e.g.: phone: stone, alone)._____
_____
_____

What are some phrases that rhyme with the topic or main character's name? (e.g.: Joe: in the snow, here below)_____
_____
_____

What are some other rhyming words or phrases you'd like to use in the story? _____
_____
_____

On the back of this page, write a funny story using the rhymes you've collected.

When you're done, read your story to a classmate. Notice the rhythm of the words as you read.

Page 38, Teaching Writing With Mentor Texts in the Primary Classroom, Copyright © 2011 by Nicole Groeneweg

Pamela Duncan Edwards

"And I do like writing alliterative books. I have great fun writing them, because I get my thesaurus out. I have to find a word that begins with that letter that will say what I want to say."

Pamela Duncan Edwards' words all but sing from the page. A former preschool teacher and school librarian in England, she comes to writing for children naturally.

Edwards often teams with illustrator Henry Cole, a match that capitalizes on their combined sense of humor. Also plain in their books is Edwards' love of nature and science. Children who read Edwards alliterative texts are bound to learn facts about nature.

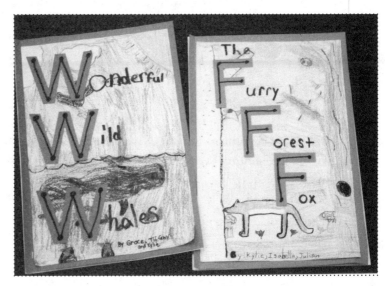

Studying the Craft: Alliteration

Sharing books written by Pamela Duncan Edwards provides an excellent opportunity for emergent readers and writers to practice beginning sounds and blends.

✮ Read aloud a variety of Pamela Duncan Edwards' books for enjoyment. (To familiarize the class with the author's work, try sharing the books over a couple of days.)

✮ Familiarize students with the term *alliteration*. Explain that this mentor author has texts alive with alliteration, a literary device in which the initial consonant, consonant blend, or on occasion, a vowel (assonance) is repeated throughout the text.

Recommended Reading

These mentor texts are sure to tickle funny bones, even while you focus students' attention on alliteration.

Clara Caterpillar
(HarperCollins, 2001)

Four Famished Foxes and Fosdyke
(HarperCollins, 1995)

Rosie's Roses
(HarperCollins, 2003)

Some Smug Slug
(HarperCollins, 1996)

The Worrywarts
(HarperCollins, 1999)

Cultivating the Writer's Notebook

Set up a Pamela Duncan Edwards writing center where students can create their own alliterative stories. Include the following materials:

- ◎ a collection of Pamela Duncan Edwards books, including *Some Smug Slug*
- ◎ stickers and stamps of alphabet letters
- ◎ letters cut from construction paper
- ◎ copy paper, lined paper, stapler for bookmaking

✰ Distribute a copy of Altogether Alliterative (page 42) to each student. Explain that students should use this prewriting page to plan their own stories that include alliteration. (See the Dynamic Mini Lesson.)

✰ Show students what items you've added to the writing center to stimulate writing with alliteration. Invite students to use colorful paper letters to set off the beginning of each word in story titles. Explain that stickers or stamps can set off the first letter of each alliterative word in the stories.

Other Resources

✰ Visit Pamela Duncan Edwards' Web site: **www.pameladuncanedwards.com**

✰ View or read the Reading Rockets interview with Pamela Duncan Edwards: **www.readingrockets.org/books/interviews/edwards**

✰ Check out illustrator Henry Cole's Web site: **www.henrycole.net**

Alliteration takes center stage in the writing center.

Standards Addressed (McREL Benchmarks Level I K–2)

- ✔ Uses writing and other methods (using letters or phonetically spelled words, telling, dictating, making lists) to describe familiar persons, places, objects, or experiences (Language Arts Standard 1: benchmark 6).

- ✔ Uses complete sentences in written compositions (Language Arts Standard 3: benchmark 2)

- ✔ Uses nouns in written compositions (e.g., singular, plural, possessive). (Language Arts Standard 3: benchmark 3)

- ✔ Uses verbs in written compositions (e.g., verbs for a variety of situations, action words). (Language Arts Standard 3: benchmark 4)

- ✔ Uses adjectives in written compositions (e.g., descriptive words). (Language Arts Standard 3: benchmark 5)

Dynamic Mini Lesson: Alliteration

Groeneweg sets up a chart for recording words beginning with S.

Groeneweg: Today we're going to reread *Some Smug Slug*. This time we're going to listen carefully for words that begin with S.

Groeneweg reads aloud Some Smug Slug. *At the end of each page she pauses and asks students to share their observations.*

Groeneweg: Did you hear any words beginning with S? Who can tell me a few?

A few students provide S words.

Groeneweg: Let's make a list to keep track of them. We'll use this chart.

Groeneweg asks volunteers to write the words they've come up with on the chart paper.

Groeneweg: I'll continue reading, and we'll all keep listening for S words.

Groeneweg reads aloud the rest of the book. Each time she encounters a word that begins with S, she records the word on the chart.

Groeneweg: Now you're going to write your own story using alliteration. I'm going to have you organize your prewriting ideas on a handout.

Groeneweg distributes a copy of Altogether Alliterative (page 42) to each student.

Name: _____ Date: _____

Altogether Alliterative

This story features words that begin with the letter ☐ .

List words below that begin with this letter. You can use a dictionary to help you find words.

Character
What are the character names? List some words that describe each character.

_____

_____

_____

_____

_____

_____

Setting
When does this story take place? List some words that name the time or day.

_____

_____

Where does this story take place? List some words that describe the setting.

_____

_____

Problem
Describe the problem or conflict in the story.

```
┌──────────────────────────────────────────┐
│                                            │
│                                            │
│                                            │
│                                            │
└──────────────────────────────────────────┘
```

Solution
Describe how the problem is resolved.

```
┌──────────────────────────────────────────┐
│                                            │
│                                            │
│                                            │
│                                            │
└──────────────────────────────────────────┘
```

For an extra challenge, circle all the nouns with blue crayon. Circle all the adjectives with green crayon.

Patricia Hubbell

"Anything can lead to a poem . . . a rhythm that gets going in my head, maybe the sound of my horse's hooves, clipclop-clippity-clopping down the road, a couple of words overheard in a conversation."

When she was ten years old, Patricia Hubbell wrote her first poem while sitting in a tree and looking at the nearby meadow. A fox began jumping and pouncing, probably chasing a mouse, but to young Patricia it looked as if he was dancing. Later that day and inspired by the scene she witnessed, Hubbell wrote *Prey Ballet*.

Since then, Patricia Hubbell has penned a multitude of poems, many of which are in published collections like *Earthmates: Poems* (Marshall Cavendish, 2006). And, lucky for us, her poetic talents are evidenced in her picture books as well.

Studying the Craft: Onomatopoeia

A literary device named for the Greek word meaning "name-making," onomatopoeia refers to words that mimic the sound they represent. Words like *whizz*, *zoom* and *rumble* make our tongues feel ticklish. Authors such as Hubbell draw on onomatopoeia and other figurative language to make their writing more vibrant.

✵ Introduce the term *onomatopoeia* by having students take walks outside and listen to the sounds in the environment (birds, cars, wind). Once back in the classroom, make a list of the sounds and how one can spell them. (See the Dynamic Mini Lesson.)

✵ When students are ready to identify onomatopoeic words, begin a shared reading activity with one of Patricia Hubbell's books. Select your own or one from the Recommended Reading list provided.

Recommended Reading

Each of these books is a treasure trove of onomatopoeia. Hubbell's newest book, *Teacher!*, is a particularly good read for setting off the beginning of a school year.

Camel Caravan
(Tambourine 1996)

Cars: Rushing! Honking! Zooming!
(Marshall Cavendish, 2006)

I Like Cats
(North-South Books, 2003)

Teacher!: Sharing, Helping, Caring
(Marshall Cavendish, 2009)

Trains: Steaming! Pulling! Huffing!
(Marshall Cavendish, 2005)

Trucks: Whizz! Zoom! Rumble!
(Marshall Cavendish, 2006)

Cultivating the Writer's Notebook

Explain that students will encounter onomatopoeic words in books, outdoor games, and other sources.

✣ Give a copy of the Collecting Sound Words (page 46) to each child. Ask students to collect and record words and add them their Writer's Notebook over time.

✣ Have students weave onomatopoeic words into their own writing. To begin, have students brainstorm words that represent sounds that airplanes make (*whir, boom, roar*). Use the words to make a book (in the style of *Cars*, *Trucks*, and *Trains*). To take the writing a step further, make a set of transportation sound books. The set could include other modes of transportation such as bikes, boats, and helicopters.

Other Resources

✣ Visit the author's Web site:
http://www.kidspoet.com/main.html

✣ Read an interview with Patricia Hubbell on the Poetry Makers series, courtesy of the blog The Miss Rumphius Effect:
http://missrumphiuseffect.blogspot.com

Students incorporate onomatopoeic words into their writing.

Standards Addressed (McREL Benchmarks Level I K–2)

✔ Drafting and Revising: Uses strategies to draft and revise written work (e.g., rereads; rearranges words, sentences, and paragraphs to improve or clarify meaning; varies sentence type; adds descriptive words and details; deletes extraneous information; incorporates suggestions from peers and teachers; sharpens the focus). (Language Arts Standard 1: benchmark 2)

✔ Editing and Publishing: Uses strategies to edit and publish written work (e.g., proofreads using a dictionary and other resources; edits for grammar, punctuation, capitalization, and spelling at a developmentally appropriate level; incorporates illustrations or photos; uses available, appropriate technology to publish work; uses legible handwriting; shares finished products). (Language Arts Standard 1: benchmark 3)

✔ Uses descriptive and precise language that clarifies and enhances ideas (e.g., concrete words and phrases, common figures of speech, sensory details). (Language Arts Standard 2: benchmark 1)

Dynamic Mini Lesson: Collecting Sound Words

Groeneweg: Yesterday we went on a walk and listened to sounds cars make. Let's read the list of sounds we heard.

Students read list of car sounds.

Groeneweg: Now listen for the sounds cars make in *Cars* by mentor author Patricia Hubbell.

Groeneweg reads the mentor text.

Groeneweg: What are some of the words Hubbell used to show cars make noise?

Groeneweg charts students' responses. Students compare and discuss the sounds.

Groeneweg: Now we're going to go on another walk. This time we'll bring a recorder with us.

Class goes for a "listening walk" outside again or around the inside the school building.

Once back in the classroom, the group charts the sounds heard and posts this list in the writing center.

Groeneweg: We've collected many sound words. There's a special word for words that sound like the sound they make. It's onomatopoeia. That's a long word for sound words!

Groeneweg hands out a copy of Collecting Sound Words (page 46) to each student.

Groeneweg: You're going to begin a collection of onomatopoeic words. Collect them on the sheet and glue it in your Writer's Notebook. Anytime you hear or think of one, you can add it to your list.

I'll leave the tape recorder along with the recordings in the writing center. Feel free to play the tape when you're doing your writing; hearing some of the sounds we've collected will encourage you.

Car Sounds

vroom
beep
honk
toot
rumble

Name: _____   Date: _____

Collecting Sound Words

List sound words, words that name the sound they make (ex.: *boom*). The words can be from your reading or from sounds you've heard. Anytime you hear or think of a sound word, add it to this list.

Weather Sounds	Vehicle Sounds
Animal Sounds	Sport Sounds
Insect Sounds	Other Sounds

Include this page in your Writer's Notebook and use words from this collection in your writing. Sound words will help make your stories especially interesting to read.

Julius Lester

"My advice for someone who wants to be a writer is to read, read, read. It is important to know what others have written. It is important to learn the possibilities of things to write about and the ways to write about them. There is no substitute for reading everything you can get your hands on."

An activist, journalist, radio broadcaster, historian, poet among many other things, Julius Lester has made a difference in the world. Children are fortunate that Lester is also a folklorist and writer. The inspiration for most of his stories is his family and African American history. "Sometimes I feel like there are all these spirits of blacks inside me, people who never had the opportunity to tell their stories, and they have chosen me to be their voice," says Lester.

Julius Lester's advice for young writers, "You must rewrite, rewrite, rewrite." What a great quote for any writing center! Julius Lester admits that he usually rewrites stories about 20 times, yet another reason to feature this mentor author in your classroom.

Studying the Craft: Similes

Julius Lester's similes relate seemingly unlike items, making his text all the more vibrant for the reader.

✭ Introduce the term *simile*. Explain that authors like Lester use the literary device to associate items using comparison words, *like* or *as*. To underscore the illustrative power of simile, ask a few volunteers to offer examples of similes. Their challenge is to make the color yellow one of the items they're comparing. (See the Dynamic Mini Lesson.)

Recommended Reading

Here are some inspiring Lester texts you can use to focus on similes.

John Henry
(Dial, 1994)

Sam and the Tigers:
A New Telling of Little Black Sambo
(Dial, 1996)

Cultivating the Writer's Notebook

After reading aloud *Sam and the Tigers* and discussing Lester's thoughtful use of simile, ask students to write their own stories that tap some of the potential of that literary device.

✭ Distribute a copy of Strong Similes (page 50) to each student. Explain that students should use the trifold to brainstorm similes. Later they can tuck the sheet into their Writer's Notebook and come back to it as a resource.

✭ To help students get started writing narratives, distribute copies of a graphic organizer such as Identifying Story Elements (page 23).

Standards Addressed (McREL Benchmarks Level I K–2)

✔ Drafting and Revising: Uses strategies to draft and revise written work (e.g., rereads; rearranges words, sentences, and paragraphs to improve or clarify meaning; varies sentence type; adds descriptive words and details; deletes extraneous information; incorporates suggestions from peers and teachers; sharpens the focus). (Language Arts Standard 1: benchmark 2)

✔ Editing and Publishing: Uses strategies to edit and publish written work (e.g., proofreads using a dictionary and other resources; edits for grammar, punctuation, capitalization, and spelling at a developmentally appropriate level; incorporates illustrations or photos; uses available, appropriate technology to publish work; uses legible handwriting; shares finished products). (Language Arts Standard 1: benchmark 3)

✔ Uses descriptive and precise language that clarifies and enhances ideas (e.g., concrete words and phrases, common figures of speech, sensory details). (Language Arts Standard 2: benchmark 1)

Other Resources

✧ Visit Julius Lester's Web site: **www.members.authorsguild.net/juliuslester**

✧ Read Lester's autobiography *On Writing for Children and Other People* (Dial, 2005).

✧ Listen to recorded music by Lester.

Students refer to their Writer's Notebooks during the writing process.

Dynamic Mini Lesson: Simile

Groeneweg draws a T-chart on chart paper. She labels the top of the chart with " . . . is like a . . . ."

Groeneweg: Today we're going to write similes. Here's an example of one of Julius Lester's similes, "A flower garden is like a candy store for bees."

Groeneweg records "A flower garden" on the left side of T-chart. She writes "a candy store for bees" on the right side.

Groeneweg: Who can tell us how a flower garden is like a candy store?

Clint: It's a place where bees find sweet stuff like pollen and nectar.

Groeneweg continues with two more examples from Julius Lester: "A magnet is like Velcro shoe laces." and "A camel is like a refrigerator."

Students discuss Lester's similes and how the comparisons help a reader.

Groeneweg: Now we're going to reread *Sam and the Tigers*. I want you to listen for examples of similes.

Groeneweg reads Sam and the Tigers. Students signal when they hear a simile. Groeneweg charts the similes on the T-chart.

Groeneweg: Some of Lester's similes are unexpected comparisons. For example, in *Sam and the Tigers* Lester describes a shirt " . . . as yellow as tomorrow" and the household staple butter " . . . as golden as a dream come true."

Groeneweg: We have a collection of Julius Lester's similes. Let's think of new comparisons and add them to our chart. Turn to a classmate beside you and develop a simile together.
Student pairs share their similes with the class.

Groeneweg: Now we're going to write some similes on trifolds that are set up like our T-chart.

Groeneweg shows a blank trifold reproducible (page 50) that kids can fill in with similes.

Groeneweg: I'm going to write the words "A fish" on the first line.

Groeneweg writes "A fish" on the first line of her trifold.

Groeneweg: At the end of that top line, I'm going to write a phrase that is slippery like a fish, but isn't a fish. I know my bubbles bottle is slimy when it spills, so I'll write the words "a bubbles bottle."

Groeneweg writes "a bubbles bottle" at the end of the first line of her trifold.

Groeneweg: Now my trifold contains a simile. It says "A fish is like a bubbles bottle." In a story I might use the simile to describe an event "The fish slithered out of my hand like a slippery bubbles bottle."

Groeneweg: When you've practice writing three similes, choose one or more to include in a story.

Groeneweg: Now you're going to write your own similes. When the trifold is complete, choose one or more similes to include in a story. You can attach the trifold page to your Writer's Notebook and use the other similes another time.

Groeneweg distributes a copy of Strong Similes (page 50) to each student and demonstrates how to fold the sheet along the dotted lines.

Name: _____

Date: _____

Strong Similes

Comparisons With Similes

	is like a	is like a	is like a	_____ is as _____ as a	_____ is as _____ as a	_____ is as _____ as a

Fold here.

Fold here.

Jonathan London

"I don't like to be limited by experience or dreams. I catch words and ideas that seem to fly through the air. Hip Cat, those two words, became a story because I heard those words as a child might. Soon I had a story in mind about a cat who plays the saxophone and wants to become a jazz musician."

It was when he had his own children that Jonathan London began writing his more than seventy published children's books, including the beloved Froggy books. A nature lover, his stories often reflect his appreciation for nature. A combination of lyrical language and humorous storylines make London's books appealing to children of all ages.

Studying the Craft: Personification

Familiarize students with the term *personification*, a literary device authors use to endow objects or animals with human characteristics. Personification is one of several types of figurative language that authors can use in their craft.

✿ Read aloud *Like Butter on Pancakes* as well as a variety of other Jonathan London books for enjoyment. (To familiarize the class with the author's work, try sharing the books over a couple of days.)

✿ Young students, who are often literal, sometimes have a difficult time comprehending the concept of personification. Therefore, it is important to take time to teach the meaning of the words *literal* and *figurative*. Once students understand those words, they are more apt to understand personification when they encounter it. In turn, they are more likely to integrate the literary device into stories they write. (See the Dynamic Mini Lesson.)

Recommended Reading

Focus on personification with any of these engaging London texts.

Hip Cat
(Chronicle, 1993)

Let the Lynx Come In
(Candlewick, 1996)

Like Butter on Pancakes
(Viking, 1995)

Loon Lake
(Chronicle, 2002)

The Owl Who Became the Moon
(Dutton, 1993)

Puddles
(Viking, 1997)

White Water
(Viking, 2001)
Written with his son, Aaron London.

Cultivating the Writer's Notebook

Explain that students will be writing a story using personification in much the same way that Jonathan London does in his stories.

✫ Give a copy of the Figuring Out Personification reproducible (page 54) to each child. Ask students to find examples of personification in their reading and then draw illustrations to show what the words literally mean and what they mean figuratively.

✫ Have students weave personification into their own writing. To get started, explain that students should use the supplies in the writing center to write and then revise their stories. When it's time to publish, challenge each student to embellish a book cover with two illustrations of his or her favorite example of personification from the book, one illustration with a literal approach and another with the intended meaning. Display all of the published books in the author center.

Standards Addressed
(McREL Benchmarks Level I K–2)

✔ Drafting and Revising: Uses strategies to draft and revise written work (e.g., rereads; rearranges words, sentences, and paragraphs to improve or clarify meaning; varies sentence type; adds descriptive words and details; deletes extraneous information; incorporates suggestions from peers and teachers; sharpens the focus). (Language Arts Standard 1: benchmark 2)

✔ Editing and Publishing: Uses strategies to edit and publish written work (e.g., proofreads using a dictionary and other resources; edits for grammar, punctuation, capitalization, and spelling at a developmentally appropriate level; incorporates illustrations or photos; uses available, appropriate technology to publish work; uses legible handwriting; shares finished products). (Language Arts Standard 1: benchmark 3)

✔ Uses descriptive and precise language that clarifies and enhances ideas (e.g., concrete words and phrases, common figures of speech, sensory details). (Language Arts Standard 2: benchmark 1)

Other Resources

✫ Read Jonathan London's Froggy books.

Dynamic Mini Lesson: Personification

Groeneweg: We're going to reread *Like Butter on Pancakes*. This time you're going to find the words that Jonathan London used to make something that is not a person do something a person would do. Here's an example: *The leaves danced in the wind.*

Jakob: Leaves can't really dance.

Groeneweg: London's sentence shows how the wind blew the leaves around. This is called personification; it's when writers give animals or objects human characteristics. Now listen to the words as I read the story. Signal by putting up your thumb when you hear personification.

Groeneweg reads aloud Like Butter on Pancakes.
Students identify personification by signaling, holding their thumbs up. Groeneweg records examples along with their page numbers on chart paper.

Groeneweg: Let's look closely at the sentence "The leaves danced in the wind." Imagine that leaves were really dancing. That would be the literal way to read the sentence.

Groeneweg writes the word literal *on the board. Groeneweg draws a picture of a leaf dancing.*

Groeneweg: What does the author mean to say with the sentence? This is the figurative meaning of the sentence.

Katie: That the leaves are being blown in the wind.

Groeneweg writes the word figurative *on the board. She draws a picture of leaves being blown in the wind.*

Groeneweg: Now, you are going to choose one of the examples from *Like Butter on Pancakes*, then draw pictures to show the literal and figurative meaning of the sentence. Do this in your Writer's Notebook. After that, you will work on the Figuring Out Personification sheet. You can also save that completed sheet in your Writer's Notebook.

Groeneweg distributes a copy of Figuring Out Personification (page 54) to each student. Students complete their drawings and then the reproducible independently.

Name: _____ Date: _____

Figuring Out Personification

I read the book _____

written by _____

This example of personification is found on page _____ .

Mentor Text: _____

_____

Draw an illustration of what the text means literally (what it actually says).

Draw an illustration of what the text means figuratively (what the mentor intends it to mean).

Eve Bunting

*"As a writer, you have to be open to what's going on—and not be afraid of it.
I think adults tend not to understand how smart children are. . . .
I think they understand more, and are more sensitive,
than an awful lot of adults give them credit for."*

A prolific writer with dozens and dozens of books for children on library and playroom bookshelves, Eve Bunting has warmed the hearts of children all over the world. She has also made them cry, made them angry, and made them worried. Eve Bunting's stories are awash with emotions.

Born in Ireland where the storytellers used to travel from house to house, sharing tales of ghosts and fairies, Eve Bunting loves a good story. She considers herself to be one of these storytellers, known as shanachies.

Studying the Craft: Writing for Effect

Whether they are feeling sad, frightened, or warm, children will certainly experience powerful emotions while reading an Eve Bunting book. In many of her works, this mentor author cleverly intertwines the story with a valuable life lesson.

Particularly emotive are Bunting's stories, *The Memory String* (Clarion, 2000), *Going Home* (HarperCollins, 1996), *I Have an Olive Tree* (HarperCollins, 1999), and *Gleam and Glow* (Harcourt, 2001). If you intend to use these titles in your classroom, pre-read the books first. Match the books to the maturity and composition of the class.

✛ Read aloud a variety of Eve Bunting's books for enjoyment. (To familiarize the class with the author's work, try sharing the books over a couple of days.)

✛ Introduce the concept of evoking readers' feelings. Ask students to brainstorm a few reasons why an author would write for effect. Invite students to discuss books they have read that appealed to their feelings. (Perhaps a beloved book helped them feel comforted, or a scary book made them feel afraid.)

Recommended Reading

From a moving journey about modern day immigrants to thoughtful tales of adoptive families, the Bunting texts cited below will help you illustrate how writing can evoke readers' feelings.

How Many Days to America
(Clarion, 1988)

Jin Woo
(Clarion, 2001)

Train to Somewhere
(Clarion, 1996)

The Wednesday Surprise
(Clarion, 1989)

✣ Label book baskets with the words *sad, happy, angry, frightened, confused,* and *frustrated.* Eve Bunting's books can be added to a basket matching the feeling the reader has after reading the book. This can be done by the class or by individual students. Discuss the feeling each book evoked in readers. If students suggest other words, add more baskets. (See the Dynamic mini Lesson.)

✣ Ask students to make stick puppets with construction paper circles mounted on tongue depressors. You can call them Feelings Faces. Explain that students should decorate the puppets faces to depict different emotions (for example: *happy, angry,* and *worried*). Invite students to turn to the Feelings Faces when doing their writing, and like Eve Bunting, they should write text that tries to evoke specific feelings in their readers.

Cultivating the Writer's Notebook

Have students choose an emotion and complete the Writing With Feeling reproducible (page 58). Use the sheet as a jumping-off point for writing a story.

✣ For an extra challenge, ask students to publish the story in a circular format that emulate the stick puppets. Students can assemble booklets with paper and cut them into circles. The book jacket may be designed as a face and depict an emotion their writing tries to bring out in the reader.

Other Resources

✣ Read a Reading Rockets interview with Eve Bunting: **www.readingrockets.org**

✣ Read an interview with Eve Bunting: **www.bookpage.com/9705bp/childrens/evebunting.html**

Standards Addressed (McREL Benchmarks Level I K–2)

✔ Uses prewriting strategies to plan written work (Language Arts Standard 1: benchmark 1).

✔ Writes in a variety of forms or genres (e.g., picture books, friendly letters, stories, poems, information pieces, invitations, personal experience narratives, messages, responses to literature). (Language Arts Standard 1: benchmark 7)

✔ Writes for different purposes (Language Arts Standard 1: benchmark 8).

Students share their Feelings Faces.

Dynamic Mini Lesson: Writing for Effect

Groeneweg: Today we're going to read *The Wednesday Surprise*. When I read something Eve Bunting has written that makes you feel sad, happy, angry or worried, show me that feeling with your facial expression. That will be your signal.

Groeneweg reads aloud The Wednesday Surprise *to the group. At emotional scenes, students show the corresponding emotion with their facial expressions.*

Groeneweg and students discuss the different emotions and what specific words and phrases in Bunting's text triggered the emotions.

Groeneweg: Now you're going to think about how Eve Bunting accomplished making you feel the way you did. We're going to look in her text to find the words and phrases she used to bring out those emotions in us, her readers.

Groeneweg distributes a copy of Writing With Feeling (page 58) to each student. Students complete the reproducible independently and use it to inspire their story writing.

Name: _____ Date: _____

Writing With Feeling

Use this story planner to help you write a story inspired by mentor author
Eve Bunting.

What feelings do you want your story to bring out in your reader?

_____

_____

**Describe how the place or setting will contribute to the
reader's feelings.**

_____

_____

Describe the problem or conflict in the story.

_____

_____

**Characters react to problems. How will the reader know what the
characters are feeling? What evidence will the reader have?**

_____

_____

**If there is a solution to this story, how does it come about? What will
happen to the problem?**

_____

_____

On the back of this page, write a draft of your story. When you're done, read your
story to a classmate. As you read watch your classmate's face for emotional reactions.
When you're done reading, discuss the story and how it made your classmate feel.
Have him or her write a sentence beneath your story that describes the effect your
story had on him or her.

Marissa Moss

"I had already published nearly a dozen books when I got the idea for Amelia's Notebook. I was buying school supplies for my son when I saw one of the black-and-white composition books. It reminded me of the notebook I had when I was a kid, so I bought it (for myself, not my son) and I wrote and drew what I remembered from when I was nine. Amelia's what came out."

Marissa Moss has wanted to write and draw since she was five. When she spotted a composition book while shopping for school supplies with her son, a light bulb went off. She could tell her story in the composition book through a diary format. That's when the idea for the Amelia series was born. Her first journal book, *Amelia's Notebook,* was followed by many more Amelia books, some historical journals, and now a new series for boys, the *Alien Eraser* series.

Children often dread writing in journals and diaries because they feel they have nothing to write. Moss's humor and voice help children change these views.

Studying the Craft: Voice

Explain that formats like journals give readers a perfect means of studying the narrative element of voice. By using journals as a format, authors can have their characters record private ideas, thoughts, notions, and other thinking. A journal is personal and private, allowing the character's point of view and voice to be readily spotted and explored.

✯ Read aloud *Amelia's Notebook* and other books by Marissa Moss for enjoyment. (To familiarize the class with the author's work, try sharing the books over a couple of days.)

✯ Have students look for evidence of point of view and voice as you read aloud entries from *Amelia's Notebook*. (See the Dynamic Mini Lesson.)

Recommended Reading

Each of the following books is an excellent example of journaling with voice. The Amelia series focuses on a girl in elementary school. The historical journals reflect a child's voice from a particular historical period. The books in the Alien Eraser series are written from a young boy's point of view.

Amelia Hits the Road
(Tricycle Press, 1997)

Amelia Lends a Hand
(American Girl, 2002)

Amelia's Family Ties
(American Girl, 2000)

Amelia's Notebook
(Tricycle Press, 1995)

***Emma's Journal:
The Story of a Colonial Girl***
(Harcourt, 1999)

***Hannah's Journal:
The Story of an Immigrant Girl***
(Harcourt, 2000)

***Max Disaster #1:
Alien Eraser to the Rescue***
(Candlewick, 2009)

***Max Disaster #2:
Alien Eraser Unravels the Mystery of
the Pyramids***
(Candlewick, 2009)

Set up a Marissa Moss author center where students can read and write journals and diaries. Include the following materials:

- ◉ Marissa Moss's journal-style books, including: the Amelia and Alien Eraser series and the historical diaries
- ◉ copies of the reproducible Journal pages (page 58)
- ◉ a collection of published journals and diaries, including: *Diary of a Spider* by Doreen Cronin (Joanna Cotler Books, 2005) and *Diary of a Wimpy Kid . . .* by Jeff Kinney (Amulet Books, 2007).
- ◉ stickers and embellishments

✫ Have students begin keeping their own Amelia-styled journals. To get started, have students clip together multiple pages of the blank Journal Page (page 62) until they're ready to bind their journals and add covers. (If you prefer, supply students with blank journals, composition books, or dollar store journals.) Note: I do believe that the students' journals should be confidential, but I need to grade them, so I explain that only I will be looking at their work. First and second graders are usually okay with this.

Standards Addressed
(McREL Benchmarks Level I K–2)

- ✔ Generates questions about topics of personal interest (Language Arts Standard 4: benchmark 1).
- ✔ Uses writing and other methods to describe familiar persons, places, objects, or experiences (Language Arts Standard 1: benchmark 6).
- ✔ Writes for different purposes (Language Arts Standard 1: benchmark 8).
- ✔ Writes expressive compositions (e.g. authentic voice). (Level 3-5, Language Arts Standard 1: benchmark 10)

Other Resources

✫ Visit Marissa Moss's Web site:
   www.marissamoss.com

Students use Amelia's Notebook
as a basis for their own journal writing.

Dynamic Mini Lesson: Voice

Groeneweg: Today we're going to read one entry from *Amelia's Notebook.* I want you to listen to words the author uses to show us who is telling the story.

Groeneweg reads aloud an excerpt from the book.

Groeneweg: Who was telling the story? Whose voice is it?

Carly: It seemed like Amelia.

Groeneweg: What evidence do we have? What words helped you figure out that Amelia was telling the story?

Amber: She said the words *I* and *my.*

Ian: I heard *mine* and *me.*

Groeneweg: Now I want you to work with a partner. Together, look through the Amelia books for a paragraph that shows evidence of Amelia's point of view. You'll record the text in your Writer's Notebook so you'll have it for future reference.

Volunteers read aloud the paragraphs they used for evidence.

Groeneweg: We know who is telling us the story in Amelia's Notebook. We know Amelia is telling us the story because we can hear her voice.

Groeneweg writes the word voice *on the board.*

Groeneweg: We can tell what Amelia's attitude and personality are like because of the words she uses and the things she says.

Groeneweg distributes a few copies of the blank Journal Pages (page 62) to each student.

Groeneweg: An author's voice is natural and comes through when they write. When you are writing your own journal, your voice will be heard. You can use these pages to create your own journal. You can write your thoughts and even draw pictures.

Name: _____ Date: _____

Jon Scieszka

"My working motto and guiding principle in writing is Never Underestimate the Intelligence of Your Audience."

Children laugh out loud when they read Jon Scieszka's hilarious stories. (Scieszka's last name is Polish and pronounced SHEH–ska. It rhymes with Fresca.)

A former teacher, Scieszka understands what makes kids want to read. Attracted to his particular sense of humor, boys will read Scieszka's books until their covers' are ragged. I have had to replace *The Stinky Cheeseman* several times! For the purposes of this book, we'll be looking at Scieszka in terms of his being a master of the twisted tale, traditional tales retold from a different point of view.

Studying the Craft: Point of View

Children typically write stories from their own point of view. It's with what they're most familiar. You can help introduce students to the narrative element known as point of view by selecting and reading aloud a variety of books told from different viewpoints. (See the Dynamic Mini Lesson.)

✵ Read aloud several of Scieska's books for enjoyment. Reading Jon Scieska's books will provide students with a glimpse of the world from an unexpected perspective. (To familiarize the class with the author's work, try sharing the books over a couple of days.)

✵ To broaden students' familiarity with different points of view, read excerpts from books by other authors that offer interesting perspectives. Here are some titles to get you started: *Two Bad Ants* by Chris Van Ahlsburg (Houghton Mifflin, 1988), *Voices in the Park* by Anthony Browne (DK Publishing, 1998), *Wolf, Wolf* by John Rocco (Hyperion, 2007), and *You Wouldn't Want to . . .* (Franklin Watts). The last is a wide-ranging series that gives an insider's perspective on fascinating, historical roles that, in the end, we'd rather not know more about (wink!).

Recommended Reading

Focus on point of view with these twisted tales. In them, the reader learns what happens after the frog kissed the princess and what the wolf was "really" thinking during his interactions with the three little pigs.

The Frog Prince, Continued
(Viking, 1991)

The True Story of the 3 Little Pigs
(Viking Kestrel, 1989)

Cultivating the Writer's Notebook

Set up a Jon Scieszka author center where students can read and write stories told from different points of view. The center may include the following materials:

- ◎ a collection of Scieszka books
- ◎ a collection of vision-altering tools (kaleidoscopes, magnifying glasses, prismatic lenses, sunglasses, telescopes, etc.)
- ◎ a collection of nonfiction books or scientific journals with photos obtained using vision-enhancing lenses (electron microscopes, satellites, endoscopic tools, night-vision cameras, etc.)

✮ Distribute a copy of Twisted Tales (page 66) to each student. Explain that students should choose an unlikely character for a common fairy tale. Students need to retell the story from that character's point of view.

✮ When students are ready, have them write, edit, and then publish their own books. Students may enjoy embellishing book jackets with drawings of the improbable character. Display all of the published books in the author center.

One student's "twisted tale" is written from the witch's perspective.

Standards Addressed (McREL Benchmarks Level I K–2)

✔ Uses prewriting strategies to plan written work (Language Arts Standard 1: benchmark 1).

✔ Drafting and Revising: Uses strategies to draft and revise written work (e.g., rereads; rearranges words, sentences, and paragraphs to improve or clarify meaning; varies sentence type; adds descriptive words and details; deletes extraneous information; incorporates suggestions from peers and teachers; sharpens the focus). (Language Arts Standard 1: benchmark 2)

✔ Editing and Publishing: Uses strategies to edit and publish written work (e.g., proofreads using a dictionary and other resources; edits for grammar, punctuation, capitalization, and spelling at a developmentally appropriate level; incorporates illustrations or photos; uses available, appropriate technology to publish work; uses legible handwriting; shares finished products). (Language Arts Standard 1: benchmark 3)

Other Resources

✮ Visit Jon Scieszka's Web site: **www.jsworldwide.com**

✮ View or read the Reading Rocket interview with Jon Scieszka: **www.readingrockets.org**

✔ Writes for different purposes (Language Arts Standard 1: benchmark 8).

✔ Writes expressive compositions (e.g. authentic voice). (Level 3-5, Language Arts Standard 1: benchmark 10)

Dynamic Mini Lesson: Point of View

The day before this lesson, Groeneweg sets the groundwork for this lesson by familiarizing students with the traditional tale of Little Red Riding Hood.

Groeneweg: We're going to talk about some stories you know about. To start, I'm going to read a traditional version of The Three Little Pigs.

Groeneweg reads aloud The Three Little Pigs.

Groeneweg: What happened in this story?

Volunteers retell the events in chronological order. Groeneweg transcribes what students recount on a T-chart she has created on chart paper. (See the Twisted Tales reproducible for an example of how to set up the chart.) The events of this traditional version of the tale are recorded on the left side of the T-chart.

Groeneweg: Now we're going to reread a different version of the same story. The title is *The True Story of the Three Little Pigs.* This time we're going to listen for the events that are told from the wolf's point of view. Give me a thumbs-up signal when you hear something that only the wolf would see, hear, taste, smell, or say.

Groeneweg reads aloud The True Story of the Three Little Pigs.

Groeneweg: What was the wolf's viewpoint compared to the three pigs?

Groeneweg records student observations on the right side of the T-chart.
The group discusses similarities and differences between the points of view.

Groeneweg: Now, I'll read aloud the traditional version of Little Red Riding Hood again.

Groeneweg reads aloud Little Red Riding Hood.

Groeneweg: You're each going to write a new version of the story on the sheet I'm giving you now. Choose one character from the traditional tale we just read to be the new main character, the character who tells the story from his or her side of things.

Groeneweg distributes a copy of the Twisted Tales reproducible (page 66) to each student.
When students are ready, have volunteers share their twisted tales. It's an opportunity for students to see how a wide range of ideas and points of view can grow from a single shared experience.

Name: _____ Date: _____

Twisted Tales

Use this page to help you plan your twisted version of a traditional tale.

The original tale is titled: _____

My version of the tale will be titled: _____

My version will be told from the point of view of : _____

Since my version is will be told by a fresh point of view, some events in the tale will differ from the original.

Original tale	Your version
Event 1	
Event 2	
Event 3	
Ending	

Keiko Kasza

"I become the character that I'm working on at that moment. I pretend that I'm a bird looking for a mother, or a pig trying to impress his girlfriend. When I'm acting, I'm a child myself."

Author and illustrator Keiko Kasza was first an artist. It was her peek into Leo Lionni's *Frederick* that intrigued Kasza and set her path in motion. She began sketching possible characters for a story. Soon the perennial favorite *The Wolf's Chicken Stew* was born.

Studying the Craft: Story Endings

Encourage students to think about story endings. Ask them why stories need endings and whether what happens at the end is important to a good story.

✫ Read aloud a variety of Kasza books for enjoyment. (To familiarize the class with the author's work, try sharing the books over a couple of days.)

✫ Introduce students to the power that a story ending has by rereading a class favorite. As you approach the ending, close the book. Explain that you've made up a new ending. When students laughingly protest, make up a new ending. Offer yet another new ending, and so on, until students prevail and you read the "real" ending aloud.

✫ Read aloud *The Wolf's Chicken Stew*. Ask students to make predictions about what will happen next as you read, and to predict the ending. Discuss the importance of endings. (See the Dynamic Mini Lesson.)

Cultivating the Writer's Notebook

Ask students to choose a story they love to read and complete the What A Great Ending! reproducible (page 70). Have the children retell the story with a different ending. Publish these with an extra large last page for the ending. Students can "supersize" the words of the ending. This will emphasize the importance of a good ending.

Recommended Reading

Any of these Kasza texts will help you spotlight story endings, especially the charming and unexpected.

Don't Laugh, Joe
(Putnam, 1997)

A Mother for Choco
(Putnam, 1992)

The Wolf's Chicken Stew
(Putnam, 1997)

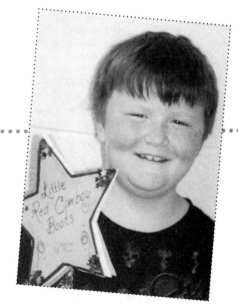

Standards Addressed
(McREL Benchmarks Level I K–2)

✔ Uses prewriting strategies to plan written work (Language Arts Standard 1: benchmark 1).

✔ Drafting and Revising: Uses strategies to draft and revise written work (e.g., rereads; rearranges words, sentences, and paragraphs to improve or clarify meaning; varies sentence type; adds descriptive words and details; deletes extraneous information; incorporates suggestions from peers and teachers; sharpens the focus). (Language Arts Standard 1: benchmark 2)

✔ Editing and Publishing: Uses strategies to edit and publish written work (e.g., proofreads using a dictionary and other resources; edits for grammar, punctuation, capitalization, and spelling at a developmentally appropriate level; incorporates illustrations or photos; uses available, appropriate technology to publish work; uses legible handwriting; shares finished products). (Language Arts Standard 1: benchmark 3)

✔ Writes for different purposes (Language Arts Standard 1: benchmark 8).

Other Resources

✰ Visit Keiko Kasza's Web site: **www.keikokasza.com**

Dynamic Mini Lesson: Story Endings

Groeneweg: Here's a book called *The Wolf's Chicken Stew* by Keiko Kasza. Look at the cover and tell me what you think might happen in the book.

Volunteers make predictions about the plot of the story.
Groeneweg begins reading aloud The Wolf's Chicken Stew. *She stops reading when the wolf arrives at the chickens' door.*

Groeneweg: What do you think will happen next?

Students make predictions.

Groeneweg: Do you think the author could end the story now?

Miles: No, because it wouldn't make sense.

Victoria: We wouldn't know what happened.

Groeneweg: Should we find out what happens at the end?

A unanimous "Yes" comes loud and clear.

Groeneweg: We're going to read to find out how this particular mentor author ended the story.

Groeneweg reads aloud the rest of The Wolf's Chicken Stew.
Students are delighted by the ending.

Groeneweg: Was the ending important to the story? How could the story have ended a different way?

Students respond, offering their observations about how the story ended.
Groeneweg guides the group in a discussion about the importance of endings, helping students come to the conclusion that a story's ending can be critical to a story's appeal.

Groeneweg: Now you're going to write an alternate ending. To get started, think about the events in the story, about what led up to the ending. Then use the What a Great Ending! sheet to help you write a new ending.

Groeneweg distributes a copy of What a Great Ending! (page 70) to each student.
Students may work in pairs or independently on this assignment.

Name: _____ Date: _____

What a Great Ending!

I read the book _____

written by _____

Describe the events at the beginning, middle, and end of the story. In the boxes, draws pictures to show what happened.

Beginning

_____

_____

_____

_____

_____

Middle

_____

_____

_____

_____

_____

End

_____

_____

_____

_____

_____

How could you make the story end in a different way? On the back of this page, write a new ending to the story.

Shirley Neitzel

"I wrote The Jacket I Wear in the Snow to show students in my class how a writer works. I used the pattern of The House That Jack Built and called it The Zipper.

A former elementary school teacher, Shirley Neitzel was inspired to write for her students. She wrote *The Jacket I Wear in the Snow* (originally the titled *The Zipper*) to show her class how a writer writes. Later, when Neitzel was asked about the gender of the main character in *The Jacket I Wear in the Snow*, Neitzel answered that she had been thinking of a boy as she wrote it. There were no clues in the text, so it was the illustrator who envisioned a girl and brought that character to light. The rest is history.

Neizel's cumulative storytelling and the rebus-style illustrations that complement the text can help students see clearly the interplay between text and illustration.

Studying the Craft: Rebus Stories

Cumulative tales and rebus stories have been a favorite children's genre for decades. In many classrooms, teachers use the repetition and illustrated rebuses to help beginning readers construct meaning. More experienced readers encounter the rebus as they practice grammar and writing skills. They learn that it is often nouns that are replaced with drawings in rebus stories. (See Dynamic Mini Lesson.)

✿ Read aloud a variety of Neitzel's books for enjoyment. (To familiarize the class with the author's work, try sharing the books over a couple of days.)

Cultivating the Writer's Notebook

Set up a Shirley Neitzel author center where students can read and write cumulative and rebus stories. The center may include the following materials:
- ⊚ a collection of Neitzel's books
- ⊚ a copy of the traditional tale The House that Jack Built and other cumulative stories, including I Knew an Old Woman Who Swallowed a Fly and *The Napping House* by Audrey Wood (Harcourt Brace, 1994)

Recommended Reading

Study the attributes of cumulative tales and rebus stories with any of these texts by Shirley Neitzel.

The House I'll Build for the Wrens (Greenwillow, 1997)

I'm Taking a Trip on My Train (Greenwillow, 1999)

The Jacket I Wear in the Snow (Greenwillow, 1989)

Our Class Took a Trip to the Zoo (Greenwillow, 2002)

Who Will I Be? A Halloween Rebus Story (Greenwillow, 2005)

⊚ rebus stories from magazines such as *Highlights* (Highlights for Children)

⊚ a collection of clothing that matches the items in *The Jacket I Wear in the Snow* (i.e., a jacket, scarf, etc.). Children can use the clothing for acting out the story.

✫ Distribute a copy of Rebus Story (page 73) to each student. Have students complete the planning sheet and then write their own cumulative stories with rebus illustrations. Ask students to make drawings or use stamps for rebus illustrations. Note: Making enlarged photocopies of the reproducible is recommended.

Standards Addressed (McREL Benchmarks Level I K–2)

✔ Uses prewriting strategies to plan written work (Language Arts Standard 1: benchmark 1).

✔ Uses writing and other methods to describe familiar persons, places, objects, or experiences (Language Arts Standard 1: benchmark 6).

✔ Writes for different purposes (Language Arts Standard 1: benchmark 8).

Other Resources

✫ Visit Shirley Neitzel's Web site for teaching ideas: **www.shirleyneitzel.com**

Dynamic Mini Lesson: Rebus Narrative

Groeneweg: Today we're going to read aloud and act out *The Jacket I Wear in the Snow*.

Groeneweg invites volunteers to portray events in the story. One volunteer will help the other volunteer put on the clothing identified in the story.

Two student volunteers (Kevin and Travis) work together to get one of them dressed appropriately.

Groeneweg: How did Kevin know what to wear?

Latrice: The pictures in the story showed him.

Groeneweg: Yes. What kinds of words did the illustrator draw?

Carmen: They're things like clothing people wear.

Groeneweg: Yes. But are they verbs? Nouns?

Zaire: They're nouns.

Groeneweg: Now you're going to write your own rebus stories using the Rebus Story worksheet.

Groeneweg distributes a copy of Rebus Story (page 73) to each student.
Students complete the reproducible with their own rebus illustrations.

Name: _____ Date: _____

Rebus Story

Write your own rebus story. Fill in the blank boxes with some of the nouns from your story, including characters, places, and objects.

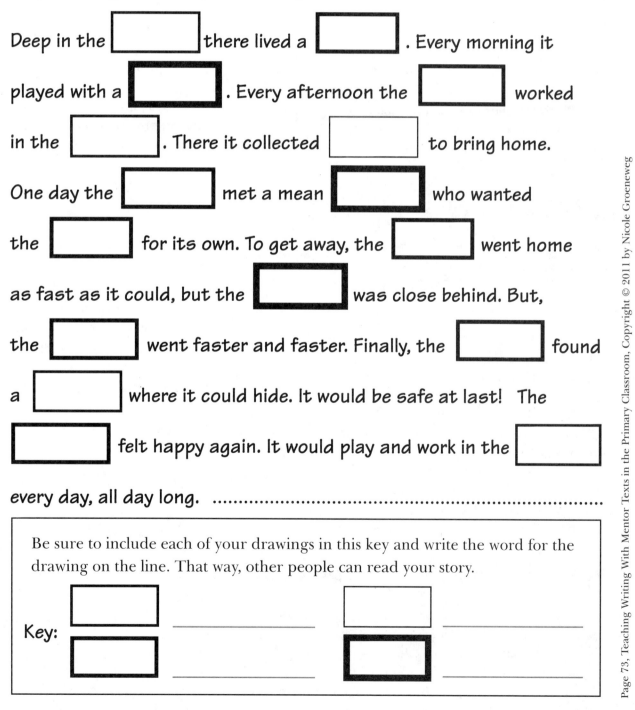

Deep in the [ ] there lived a [ ]. Every morning it

played with a [ ]. Every afternoon the [ ] worked

in the [ ]. There it collected [ ] to bring home.

One day the [ ] met a mean [ ] who wanted

the [ ] for its own. To get away, the [ ] went home

as fast as it could, but the [ ] was close behind. But,

the [ ] went faster and faster. Finally, the [ ] found

a [ ] where it could hide. It would be safe at last! The

[ ] felt happy again. It would play and work in the [ ]

every day, all day long. ....

Be sure to include each of your drawings in this key and write the word for the drawing on the line. That way, other people can read your story.

Key: [ ] _____   [ ] _____

[ ] _____   [ ] _____

Alma Flor Ada

> "...that's what's exciting about being bicultural. To be able to do it well in one language and to do it well in the other language. It's like moving from two very different places, like at the beach and in the mountains. You do different things in the two places. And the good thing is to be able to do both."

Alma Flor Ada, who has written numerous children's books of poetry, narrative fiction, folklore, and nonfiction, provides her readers with text that is rich with multicultural details.

As we turn to Alma Flor Ada as a mentor author, we set our sights on the ways in which she has masterfully intertwined several classic fairy tales into an entertaining epistolary for young children. To accomplish her task, Ada created fractured fairy tales—adaptations of the traditional tales. Using letters of correspondence between celebrated fairy tale characters, Ada provides readers with high-interest, atypical points of view.

Studying the Craft: Epistolary

Epistolary is a narrative element that enables authors to tell a story through a series of letters. It's a powerful tool for a writer to give the reader differing points of view in a narrative.

✫ Read aloud a variety of Alma Flor Ada's books for enjoyment. (To familiarize the class with the author's work, try sharing the books over a couple of days.)

✫ Introduce the format of the friendly letter. Read aloud *Dear Peter Rabbit*. (See Recommended Reading list). Ask volunteers to describe different parts of a letter (heading/ salutation, body, closing, signature). On a sheet of chart paper, record the name of each part and where it is located. Post the completed chart in a highly-visible location. (See the Dynamic Mini Lesson.)

Recommended Reading

Alma Flor Ada uses correspondence to show readers how different characters view events happening in the Hidden Forest.

Dear Peter Rabbit
(Atheneum, 1994)

With Love, Little Red Hen
(Atheneum, 2001)

Yours Truly, Goldilocks
(Atheneum, 1998)

Cultivating the Writer's Notebook

Set up a writing center focused on letter writing. Include the following:
- ◎ a collection of Alma Flor Ada books, including *Dear Peter Rabbit*
- ◎ a sheet of chart paper with the parts of a friendly letter clearly labeled
- ◎ materials for letter writing (Dollar store stationery works well.)

- ◎ postcards (Multiple copies of page 76 work well.)
- ◎ greeting cards (or craft paper and supplies to make cards)
- ◎ stickers (to use as postage stamps)
- ◎ a mailbox (Invite volunteers to create one using a shoebox.)

✰ Have students create a collaborative class book. Explain that each student will write a friendly letter or postcard from the perspective of one of the fairy tale characters they read about in the Alma Flor Ada texts. The correspondence will be one character writing to another. After students have written and embellished them with illustrations, compile the class correspondence into a book (perhaps entitled *Sincerely, Little Red Riding Hood* or another appropriate title).

Other Resources

✰ Visit Alma Flor Ada's Web site: **www.almaflorada.com**

✰ View the video *Alma Flor Ada*: **www.delsolbooks.com**

Standards Addressed (McREL Benchmarks Level I K–2)

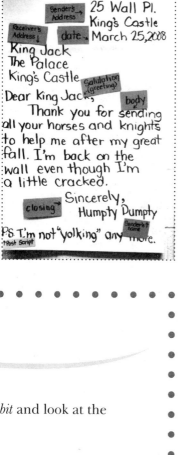

✔ Uses prewriting strategies to plan written work (Language Arts Standard 1: benchmark 1)

✔ Uses writing and other methods to describe familiar persons, places, objects, or experiences. (Language Arts Standard 1: benchmark 6)

✔ Writes in a variety of forms or genres (e.g., picture books, friendly letters, stories, poems, information pieces, invitations, personal experience narratives, messages, responses to literature). (Language Arts Standard 1: benchmark 7)

✔ Writes for different purposes. (Language Arts Standard 1: benchmark 8)

Dynamic Mini Lesson:

Groeneweg writes one of the letters from Dear Peter Rabbit *on chart paper.*

Groeneweg: We're going to reread one of the letters from *Dear Peter Rabbit* and look at the different parts of a letter. What do you see at the top of the letter?

Owen: There's the date.

Groeneweg: It's part of the heading. The date and the address are part of the heading.

Groeneweg labels the heading with a different color marker then continues with the rest of the parts (the salutation, the body, the closing, the signature). Finally, she posts the labeled letter in the writing center.

Groeneweg: Now you're going to write a postcard to a classmate or buddy. Remember to include all the parts of a letter. You can put your postcard in the mailbox. We'll deliver them tomorrow during Reading Workshop.

Postcard Front

Greetings from

_____

(Write the name of your setting.)

(Draw a picture of your setting.)

Fold ▶ ◀ Fold

Postcard Back

Send to:

_____

_____

_____

Signed,

_____

_____

_____

_____

_____

_____

The place is great!

Dear _____

Date _____

Steven Kellogg

"I'm constantly rethinking, refining, reworking, rearranging. That's the process by which the book finds its right momentum from beginning to end."

Steven Kellogg began his storytelling career as a child, spending hours with his younger sisters drawing stories on paper. They called this special time "Telling Stories on Paper."

Since then, Kellogg has come to believe that words are like music on paper. Together his illustrations and words magically seem to bring stories to life for children. While Kellogg writes on a wide range of topics, it is his retellings of tall tales that work especially well as showcases for *hyperbole*, a literary device that's derived from exaggeration.

Studying the Craft: Hyperbole

Exaggeration is commonplace in children's retellings of events. They tend to sensationalize even the smallest of details in their oral interplay. In writing, it is more difficult to convey ideas through exaggeration for young writers.

- Read aloud a variety of Steven Kellogg's books, including *Paul Bunyan*, for enjoyment. (To familiarize the class with the author's work, try sharing the books over a couple of days.)
- Introduce the literary device known as *hyperbole*. Identify examples of it in Kellogg's books and then, as a group, take it further. Ask volunteers to find a different example of hyperbole in the text and expand on it, making the exaggeration even more outrageous. In this way, students will gain a taste for building the hyperbole and learn to apply it in the context of a story.
- To be sure students understand the concept of hyperbole, read *Paul Bunyan* aloud and ask students to identify instances of hyperbole. (See the Dynamic Mini Lesson.)

Recommended Reading

Steven Kellogg's tall tales provide excellent examples of hyperbole.

Johnny Appleseed: A Tall Tale (Morrow, 1988)

Mike Fink: A Tall Tale (Morrow, 1992)

Paul Bunyan: A Tall Tale (Morrow, 1984)

Pecos Bill: A Tall Tale (Morrow, 1986)

Cultivating the Writer's Notebook

Set up a Tall Tales center where students can read and write tall tales. This center may include the following materials:

- a collection of tall tales by Steven Kellogg
- a collection of nonfiction books on real people who inspired the tales
- materials to publish the tales (bulletin board paper, adding machine tape, lined paper, etc.)

✦ Have students weave hyperbole into their own writing. To begin, have students complete the Tall Tales Planner reproducible (page 80). On it, they will be asked to identify key details about the tall tale they intend to write, including how they will be using hyperbole in their writing.

When students are ready to publish their writing, have them trace their own bodies on bulletin board paper and cut out the silhouette. They can then embellish the pictures by drawing clothing and accoutrement to match the main character of their tall tale. For another twist, have students publish their writing on lengths of adding machine tape. Attach the ending of the story to a tongue depressor or cardboard tube and then roll up the paper. The beginning will appear on top. These tales will be tall!

Other Resources

✦ Visit Steven Kellogg's Web site: **www.stevenkellogg.com**

✦ Read or view an interview with Steven Kellogg at Reading Rockets: **www.readingrockets.org**

Standards Addressed (McREL Benchmarks Level I K–2)

✔ Drafting and Revising: Uses strategies to draft and revise written work (e.g., rereads; rearranges words, sentences, and paragraphs to improve or clarify meaning; varies sentence type; adds descriptive words and details; deletes extraneous information; incorporates suggestions from peers and teachers; sharpens the focus). (Language Arts Standard 1: benchmark 2)

✔ Editing and Publishing: Uses strategies to edit and publish written work (e.g., proofreads using a dictionary and other resources; edits for grammar, punctuation, capitalization, and spelling at a developmentally appropriate level; incorporates illustrations or photos; uses available, appropriate technology to publish work; uses legible handwriting; shares finished products). (Language Arts Standard 1: benchmark 3)

Students share the illustration that accompanies their tall tale.

Dynamic Mini Lesson: Hyperbole

Groeneweg: Today we're going to reread *Paul Bunyan* to find text that is exaggerated. We're going to look for parts of the story where the author wanted to emphasize a character's size or skill or make something more amazing or memorable.

Groeneweg: Here is an example: *I'm so hungry I could eat a horse.* I might be hungry, but I couldn't really eat a whole horse. Authors use exaggeration or hyperbole to make readers take notice of a big, hungry, or strong character. I'll read the story aloud. Signal with a thumbs-up when you think mentor author Steven Kellogg is using exaggeration.

Groeneweg highlights or marks the text after receiving each signal. Then continues reading and waiting for signals from students.

After reading, Groeneweg invites students to discuss each exaggeration found in the tale, each section of text the students drew attention to by signaling.

Groeneweg: Why do you think Steven Kellogg exaggerated how big Paul Bunyan was?

Groeneweg and students discuss some of the ways in which tall tales entertained (and buoyed up) frontier folk.

Groeneweg: Tall tales were told in part to lift people's spirits when times were tough. Storytellers made the main characters even more extraordinary.

Shawn: Like my grandfather's fish tales. He's always telling stories that sound like tall tales.

Groeneweg: Yes! Now you're going to write an original tall tale using the planning page I'm handing out now.

Groeneweg distributes a copy of the Tall Tales Planner (page 80) to each student.

Students complete the planning page with key information and illustrations, and then write their first drafts on the back of the sheet.

Name: _____ Date: _____

Tall Tales Planner

Finish these sentences.

My tall tale is about a person named _____

This person lived in _____

People knew this person was different from other people because

_____

_____

_____

_____

_____ could do amazing things other people couldn't do, such as

_____

_____

_____

_____

This person is most remembered for _____

_____

_____

_____

Some people say that _____ in my tale was responsible for

_____

On the back of this page, write a tall tale using the answers you wrote above. Use a yellow marker to highlight where you've included hyperbole.

James Marshall

"If I don't have a good character, then I don't have a book."

James Marshall was a prolific writer and illustrator, the author of more than 80 books for children. His humor is evident in series that grew out *Miss Nelson Is Missing* (Houghton Mifflin, 1977), *George and Martha* (Houghton Mifflin, 1972), and *The Cutups* (Viking Kestrel, 1984).

Have children look for fat cats and piles of things ready to tip over as they read James Marshall's books. He often slipped these amusing images into his illustrations. Since he was born and raised in Texas, Texan things are sprinkled throughout the Miss Nelson series.

Studying the Craft: Fairy Tale Features

James Marshall's illustrations and humorous retellings of favorite fairy tales make him an ideal fairy tale mentor for young children.

✫ Read aloud a variety of James Marshall books for enjoyment. Ask the children to listen for features of fairy tales. Ask: What hints does the author give us that the story you're reading is a fairy tale? (To familiarize the class with the author's work, try sharing the books over a couple of days.)

✫ Introduce the concept of fairy tale features. (See below.) Read aloud Marshall's retelling of Little Red Riding Hood. (See *Red Riding Hood* on the Recommended Reading list.) Write the following categories on chart paper: Beginning of the Story, Heroes and Villains, Magic, Odd Numbers, Ending of the Story. After reading, invite volunteers to point out evidence of those fairy tale features from the story. Record students' observations on chart paper. (See the Dynamic Mini Lesson.)

Recommended Reading

Spotlight elements of the fairy tale genre with any of these celebrated retellings by Marshall:

Goldilocks and the Three Bears
(Dial, 1988)

Hansel and Gretel
(Dial, 1990)

James Marshall's Cinderella
(Dial, 2001)
Retold by Barbara Karlin.

Red Riding Hood
(Dial, 1987)

The Three Little Pigs
(Dial, 1989)

Beginning of the Story

"Once upon a time . . .", "One day . . .", and "A long time ago . . ." are phrases that begin most fairy tales. This element is highly apparent in James Marshall's retellings. Posting a list of such phrases around a fairy tale center will give children a resource for beginning their own fairy tale.

Heroes and Villains

There is a hero and villain in every fairy tale and children always identify with the "good guy." The villains in Marshall's fairy tales have facial expressions that would make anyone shiver, but as in all good fairy tales, the hero wins in the end.

Magic

Magic often appears in fairy tales as well. Cinderella's fairy godmother, the witch's gingerbread house, and talking wolves are a few of the examples that Marshall includes in his stories.

Other Resources

✿ Listen to an interview with James Marshall: **http://www.hbook.com/history/radio/marshall.asp** (Horn Book Radio Review)

✿ View a video tribute by friends and colleagues for the late James Marshall at **http://mitworld.mit.edu/video/637**

Odd Numbers

Sets of threes, fives, and sevens can be noted in many fairy tales. The three pigs set off into the world, the three bears take a walk while their porridge cools, and Little Red Riding Hood makes three observations about the wolf's unusual attributes.

Ending of the Story

The villain usually receives his just punishment at the end of a fairy tale, whereas the hero or heroes typically ". . . live happily ever after." Children feel satisfied with such endings and enjoy incorporating them at the conclusion of their own fairy tales.

Cultivating the Writer's Notebook

Set up a fairy tale center where students can read and write fairy tales. Include the following materials:

- ◎ a collection of James Marshall's books, including *Red Riding Hood* and *The Three Little Pigs*
- ◎ a collection of fairy tales retold by other authors
- ◎ a collection of props (wand, pot, apron, broom, etc.)
- ◎ puppets for reenacting stories
- ◎ copy paper, lined paper, stapler for book pages
- ◎ glue, glitter, plastic jewels, foil, ribbons, and other notions for decorating book covers

✿ Distribute a copy of the Fairy Tale Planner sheet (page 84) to each student. Explain that students should use the planner to identify the specifics of their particular fairy tales.

✿ When students are ready, have them write, edit, and then publish their own fairy tales. Students may enjoy embellishing book covers with drawings of their favorite fairy tale feature or portraits of the hero or villain.

Standards Addressed (McREL Benchmarks Level I K–2)

✔ Uses prewriting strategies to plan written work (Language Arts Standard 1: benchmark 1).

✔ Uses strategies to organize written work (e.g., includes a beginning, middle, and ending; uses a sequence of events). (Language Arts Standard 1: benchmark 5)

✔ Writes in a variety of forms or genres (e.g., picture books, friendly letters, stories, poems, information pieces, invitations, personal experience narratives, messages, responses to literature). (Language Arts Standard 1: benchmark 7)

✔ Writes for different purposes (Language Arts Standard 1: benchmark 8).

Dynamic Mini Lesson: Fairy Tale Features

Groeneweg writes the following categories on chart paper: Beginning of the Story, Heroes and Villains, Magic, Odd Numbers, Ending of the Story.

Groeneweg: We're going to read a couple of fairy tales retold by James Marshall. When we come to a part of the story that lets us know it's a fairy tale, we're going to add it to a list. Signal with a thumbs-up when you hear a fairy tale element.

Groeneweg reads aloud Red Riding Hood *and pauses when students signal. Groeneweg records student observations on the chart.*

Groeneweg: Now we're going to read Marshall's *The Three Little Pigs*. Signal when you hear a fairy tale element.

Groeneweg reads The Three Little Pigs *and adds more student observations to the chart.*

Groeneweg: Now you are going to use the information to help you write your own fairy tale. Think of your ideas and complete the fairy tale planning sheet.

Groeneweg distributes a copy of the Fairy Tale Planner (page 84) to each student. Students complete the reproducible independently and use it to inspire their story writing.

> **Fairy Tale Features**
> Beginning of the Story
> Heroes and Villains
> Magic
> Odd Numbers
> Ending of the Story

Name:_____ Date: _____

Fairy Tale Planner

Title: _____

Lead: How will your story begin? _____

_____

Hero/Heroine: _____

Villain: _____

Other Characters: _____

Setting:_____

Problem: _____

_____

_____

_____

_____

Magical items: _____

Odd number: _____

Resolution: How will your story end?_____

_____

_____

Draw a picture
of an important
event you plan to
include in the story.

Gail Gibbons

"...I find an expert, someone who knows a lot about the subject I'm writing about. That way I'm sure to get the most up-to-date information."

Gail Gibbons was convinced to write children's books by children themselves. Since then, she has written and illustrated more than 135 nonfiction books for children on a wide variety of topics.

Her nonfiction books enthrall young children with appealing illustrations that supplement the text and with sidebars brimming with rich details

Studying the Craft: Nonfiction Features

Nonfiction text has unique features that set it apart from the narratives stories children often read and write.

✷ Read aloud a variety of books by Gail Gibbons for enjoyment. (To familiarize the class with the author's work, try sharing the books over a couple of days.) Features found in these nonfiction books include captions, labels, pronunciation keys, maps, graphs, highlighted text, and time lines. For ideas about introducing these features, see the Dynamic Mini Lesson.

✷ To give students practice working with nonfiction text, have pairs of students work together to read one of the books from the Recommended Reading list or other nonfiction books you've selected. Ask pairs of students to work together to find and identify key features in the text and record them on their Type and Text Features sheet (page 88). Completed sheets can be stored in their Writer's Notebooks for future reference.

Cultivating the Writer's Notebook

Set up a nonfiction writing center, where students can create their own books inspired by the genre. This center may include the following materials:

◎ a collection of nonfiction books by Gail Gibbons
◎ a collection of nonfiction texts in a variety of formats, including magazines and brochures

Recommended Reading

Here are some favorite Gibbons texts you can use to focus on features of nonfiction.

Bats
(Holiday House, 1999)
Includes labels.

Dinosaurs
(Holiday House, 1987)
Includes pronunciation keys.

The Honey Makers
(Morrow, 1997)
Includes captions.

Marshes and Swamps
(Holiday House, 1999)
Includes maps.

The Moon Book
(Holiday House, 1997)
Includes time lines.

Tell Me, Tree:
All About Trees for Kids
(Little Brown, 2002)
Includes highlighted text.

- a class-generated list of nonfiction text features recorded on chart paper
- materials to highlight or indicate text features
- copy paper, lined paper, stapler for assembling nonfiction formats

✸ Have students build nonfiction writing into their repertoire. To get started on this independent writing activity, ask each student to select a topic that he or she knows a lot about already. As a group, brainstorm a list of topics and record them on chart paper. Topics might include music, clothes, cell phones, video games, basketball, the mall, and so on.

Tell students that the next step is for them to determine what format best suits their topic. For example, a nonfiction piece about clothes might work as a magazine article. A brochure format might be suitable for a piece about the mall.

When it's time to publish, challenge each student to include the type and text features you've discussed as a group and have recorded on chart paper. Invite volunteers to share their nonfiction pieces and display them in the writing center.

Standards Addressed
(McREL Benchmarks Level I K–2)

✔ Uses writing and other methods to describe familiar persons, places, objects, or experiences (Language Arts Standard 1: benchmark 6).

✔ Writes in a variety of forms or genres (e.g., picture books, friendly letters, stories, poems, information pieces, invitations, personal experience narratives, messages, responses to literature). (Language Arts Standard 1: benchmark 7).

✔ Writes for different purposes (Language Arts Standard 1: benchmark 8).

Other Resources

✸ Visit Gail Gibbons's Web site for free, downloadable teachers' guides: **www.gailgibbons.com**

✸ Find ideas in *Unwrapping a Book: Using Nonfiction to Teach Writing in the Primary Classroom* by N. Groeneweg (Creative Teaching Press, 2006)

Explorations into text features support student forays into writing nonfiction.

Dynamic Mini Lesson: Nonfiction Text Features

After introducing students to nonfiction text content in reading workshop, Groeneweg begins a mini lesson on text features.

Groeneweg: Let's review what we know about nonfiction.

Chelsea: It's real information.

Eric: It really happened.

Groeneweg: What are some of the things we see in nonfiction books that may not be fiction books?

Tanisha: Bold words.

Alison: Captions and labels.

Groeneweg: As we read *The Honey Makers,* we're going to look closely at the captions.

Groeneweg reads aloud The Honey Makers. *She pauses to point out and read aloud the captions.*

Groeneweg: What did the captions tell us?

Neil: They give us important details.

Groeneweg: Now let's work together to come up with a good definition for captions. Who can get us started with the definition?

Together, student volunteers and Groeneweg collaborate to shape a workable definition, and Groeneweg records it on chart paper. Later she'll post it in the writing center where students can see it clearly. (Over time, the chart will contain more than a dozen definitions to which students may refer.)

Groeneweg distributes a copy of Type and Text Features (page 88) to each student. She explains that over the next few days, as a group they will develop a definition for each nonfiction feature on the reproducible. Students need to record each definition as it is developed and, ultimately, attach their completed page to their Writer's Notebooks for future reference.

Over a course of a few days, Groeneweg offers a mini lesson about type treatments and text features. She invites volunteers to shape workable definitions and then records them on chart paper.

Name:_____ Date: _____

Type and Text Features

I read the book_____

written by_____

What nonfiction text features did the author use: _____

_____

_____

Next to each feature you find, write the page number where you found it.

TYPE			
bold text	color text	*italicized text*	<u>underlined text</u>
captions	fact boxes	graphs	illustrations
labeled diagrams	maps	time lines	_____

Page 88, Teaching Writing With Mentor Texts in the Primary Classroom, Copyright © 2011 by Nicole Groeneweg

Ann L. Burckhardt

Ann L. Burckhardt knows about food! She is a former reporter, columnist, and editor for the "Taste" section of the *Star Tribune*. Among her published works are several cookbooks and a series of books about cuisine around the world. Other books by Burckhardt, written especially for children, work well as models of nonfiction texts and look at food from a more socio-agricultural perspective.

Studying the Craft: Nonfiction Text Organization

Students can learn to incorporate indexes, glossaries, and tables of contents into their own nonfiction writing after studying nonfiction mentor texts.

✢ Read aloud a variety of Ann L. Burckhardt's books for enjoyment. (To familiarize the class with the author's work, try sharing the books over a couple of days.)

✢ Explain that while authors of all genres use structure to create stories, writers of nonfiction use specific organizational tools to help readers find information easily. Help students draw on what they already know. Take a picture walk through one of Burckhardt's children's books and invite students to make observations about the way the book is organized. (See the Dynamic Mini Lesson.)

Cultivating the Writer's Notebook

Set up a Pumpkins center, an area where students can read fiction and nonfiction about pumpkins. This center may include the following materials:
- ◎ a collection of Anne L. Burckhardt books
- ◎ a collection of fiction and nonfiction books about pumpkins
- ◎ a collection of pumpkins and other vegetables in a variety of sizes, shapes, and colors
- ◎ copy paper, lined paper, pumpkin-shaped cut outs, and a stapler for assembling booklets

✢ Tell students that they will use planning sheets to organize their own informational books. When students are ready, distribute a copy of Nonfiction Organizers (pages 92 through 95) to each student. After completing the graphic organizers, ask students to attach the pages to their Writer's Notebooks and begin the process of writing the story.

Recommended Reading

Students will be able to examine tables of contents, indexes, and glossaries in these simple, fact-based Burckhardt texts.

Apples
Written with reading consultant, Julia Daly.
(Bridgestone, 1996)

Corn
Written with reading consultant, Robin Johnston.
(Bridgestone, 1996)

Potatoes
Written with reading consultant, Chuck Kostichka.
(Bridgestone, 1996)

Pumpkins
(Bridgestone, 1996)

Standards Addressed
(McREL Benchmarks Level I K–2)

✔ Uses writing and other methods to describe familiar persons, places, objects, or experiences (Language Arts Standard 1: benchmark 6).

✔ Writes in a variety of forms or genres (e.g., picture books, friendly letters, stories, poems, information pieces, invitations, personal experience narratives, messages, responses to literature). (Language Arts Standard 1: benchmark 7).

✔ Writes for different purposes (Language Arts Standard 1: benchmark 8).

Other Resources

✿ Read more about Ann L. Burckhardt: **www.jacketflap.com/persondetail.asp?person=8907**

A student uses what he's learned about organizing information to create a table of contents.

Dynamic Mini Lesson: Table of Contents

Groeneweg: Today we're going to use the information we learn reading *Pumpkins* to make a table of contents.

Groeneweg reads aloud Pumpkins *by Ann L. Burckhardt. At the end of each page, she pauses to discuss the new vocabulary or information on that page. Groeneweg records each of these pieces of information (i.e., gourd, tradition, pumpkin) on a sticky note along with the page number where it was found. She sets them in no particular order on a sheet of chart paper.*

Groeneweg: Now let's look at table of contents in nonfiction books and see how authors organize them.

Students examine tables of contents in nonfiction books, including those by Burckhardt.

Groeneweg: What do you notice about the organization of the table of contents?

Maya: The pages are in order.

Nikolas: There are titles listed and then the page numbers are listed.

Groeneweg: Let's arrange these in sticky notes in numerical order to create a table of contents. Afterward, we'll use what learned to make a sample Table of Contents for your Writer's Notebooks. I will give each of you a sheet you can use to stay organized.

Students take turns arranging the sticky notes. They set them in order by page number on chart paper.

Groeneweg writes Table of Contents on the chart paper above the ordered sticky notes. If there are several sticky notes for the same page number, Groeneweg discusses how to generalize or pick main topics.
Students complete the Table of Contents reproducible (page 92).
Groeneweg retains the sticky notes for a lesson on making an index and another on assembling a glossary.

Groeneweg repeats the same format with a mini lesson about creating an index.
She invites volunteers to order the sticky notes alphabetically on the chart paper.
Students demonstrate understanding by completing the Index reproducibles (pages 93 and 94).
Note: Making double-sided photocopies of the reproducible is recommended.

Groeneweg repeats the same format with a mini lesson about creating a glossary.
She invites volunteers to put the sticky notes in alphabetical order on the chart paper.
Students demonstrate understanding by completing the Glossary reproducible (page 95).

Name: _____ Date: _____

Table of Contents

TOPIC   PAGE

_____   _____

_____   _____

_____   _____

_____   _____

_____   _____

_____   _____

_____   _____

_____   _____

_____   _____

_____   _____

_____   _____

_____   _____

_____   _____

Name: _____ Date: _____

Index

A	B	C	D
_____	_____	_____	_____
_____	_____	_____	_____
_____	_____	_____	_____
_____	_____	_____	_____
_____	_____	_____	_____
_____	_____	_____	_____

E	F	G	H
_____	_____	_____	_____
_____	_____	_____	_____
_____	_____	_____	_____
_____	_____	_____	_____
_____	_____	_____	_____
_____	_____	_____	_____

I	J	K	L
_____	_____	_____	_____
_____	_____	_____	_____
_____	_____	_____	_____
_____	_____	_____	_____
_____	_____	_____	_____

CONTINUED . . .

Name: _____ Date: _____

Index

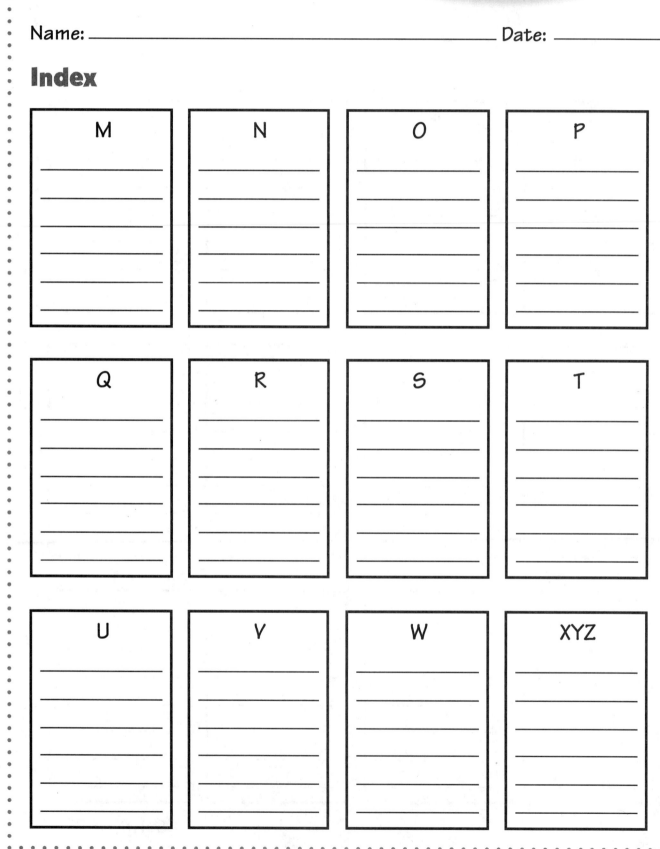

Name: _____ Date: _____

Glossary

Write the list in alphabetical order.   Provide a brief definition.

_____   _____

_____

_____   _____

_____

_____   _____

_____

_____   _____

_____

_____   _____

_____

_____   _____

_____

_____   _____

_____

Bibliography

Calkins, L. (1994). *The Art of Teaching Writing*. Portsmouth, NH: Heinemann.

Culham, R. (2003). *6+1 Traits of Writing*. New York: Scholastic.

Hyerle, D. (1996). *Visual Tools for Constructing Knowledge*. Alexandra, VA: ASCD.

Preller, J. (2001). *The Big Book of Picture Book Authors and Illustrators*. NY: Scholastic.

Shalaway, L. (2005). *Learning to Teach . . . Not Just for Beginners*. NY: Scholastic.

Serafini, F. *(2001). The Reading Workshop: Creating Space for Readers*. Portsmouth, NH: Heinemann.

Temple, C. ,Nathan, R., Burris, N., Temple, F. (1982). *The Beginnings of Writing*. Newton, MA: Allyn and Bacon.

Zaragoza, N. (2002). *Rethinking Language Arts*. New York: RoutledgeFalmer.